THE RUNNER'S BIBLE

THE RUNNER'S BIBLE

Spiritual Guidance
for
People On The Run

Compiled and Annotated
by
Nora Holm

With an Introduction
by
Polly Berrien Berends

"Write the vision and make it plain upon tables
that he may run that readeth it."
—Habakkuk 2:2

I-Level
Acropolis Books, Publisher
Lakewood, Colorado • Austell, Georgia

The Runner's Bible
Spiritual Guidance
for
People On The Run
First Acropolis Books Edition 1998

Published by Acropolis Books, Publisher,
under its *I*-Level Imprint.
All rights reserved.
Printed in the United States of America.

For information contact:
Acropolis Books, Inc.
Lakewood, Colorado

http://www.acropolisbooks.com

Cover design by Bren Frisch

Library Of Congress Cataloging-In-Publication Data

Bible. English. Authorized. Selections. 1998.
    The runner's Bible: spiritual guidance for people on the run /
compiled and annotated by Nora Holm
        p.   cm.
    Originally published: New York: Crossroad, 1993.
    ISBN 1-889051-27-6 (pbk. : alk. paper)
    1. Bible—Quotations.   I. Holm, Nora, b. 1864.   II. Bible.
English. Revised. Selections. 1998. III. Title
    [BS432.H59 1998]
    220.5' 2036—DC21   97–46190
                                                         CIP

This book is printed on acid free paper that meets
standard Z 39.48 of the American National Standards Institute

Both the King James and the English Revised Version (E.R.V.) are used in this compilation. References in parentheses indicate source of idea when not direct or continuous quotation.

Table of Contents

Statements of Truth

Table of Contents

The Divine Commands

Table of Contents

"The greatest" is the one who has the clearest
understanding of the Truth. He sees every man
as a part of his own life and serves him as though
he served himself.

Forgiveness cannot do its work upon a mind
that is poisoning itself by holding resentment.

Promises

There is no virtue in being weighted down
with the memories of past sins. Knowledge
of the Truth relieves one of all burdens.

With God nothing is impossible.

Godlikeness is revealed in perfection.
Ill health is not the Word of God, neither
His dispensation.

None other power than His must we recognize.

Table of Contents

INTRODUCTION

The Runner's Bible is one of the best pocket-sized biblical/spiritual aids for daily prayerful living I know. Not many people have heard of it, and booksellers have often assumed it is for joggers. Nevertheless, there have been over 70 printings of this gem of a book, thanks to the word of mouth of its faithful underground.

A compilation of biblical quotes and the author's own wise, inspired commentary, *The Runner's Bible* is a spiritual oxygen tank, infirmary, and compass for revivifying, healing, and reorienting busy, searching souls. Most whom come to know *The Runner's Bible* keep multiple copies—in desk drawer, briefcase, purse, bedside table, glove compartment, and bathroom—for frequent access to guidance from beyond the overwhelming interpersonal din.

Habitual use of *The Runner's Bible* reveals prayer to be not merely something some do, but as *the way to see and to be*. The God encountered there is not a hypothetical far-off superperson, but an intimate, immediate presence and underlying source and force of personal being. As a psychotherapist I find this book enormously helpful to clients, sustaining them between sessions and greatly enriching our psychospiritual work together. *The Runner's Bible* is not a substitute for the psychological help that many who seek the fullness of individual being choose in the course of a lifetime, but it is a supplemental resource, a spiritual pocket compass that can aid us immeasurably in our journey. I have personally relied on it for over 25 years of spiritual support. As a parent I watched it launch my teenage sons on their own firsthand spiritual path. I know of no other small book that is so consistently helpful.

The Runner's Bible was prepared in 1910 by Nora Holm for her on-the-run 17 year old daughter, but it is of great value of people of all ages, especially in our fast-paced society. For those familiar or unfamiliar with the *Bible* this book provides access to the true, existential value of scripture in daily life. Organized around such themes as love, thanks, healing, forgiveness, and reassurance it can be sought in moments of particular need. But just as a frequently checked compass prevents one from getting lost, regular and frequent use of *The Runner's Bible* can also help to keep us from spiritually walking off cliffs and stumbling into ditches.

I recommend random reading of only one or two brief passages at a time, followed by a short period of prayer and meditation. Open, read what your eye falls on, and then consider what this passage might have to do with you and your life in the present moment. What does it reveal about your preoccupations? Are you resentful? fearful? overexcited? What redirection does it offer? After a few moments of such reflection continue your prayer with living prayer by going forth to live your life in the light of what you have understood.

I'd like to caution against a possible misuse of *The Runner's Bible* in the form of positive thinking. Positive thinking may break the spell of negative thinking and allow divine healing to get through, but belief in the power of the conscious human psyche can also block healing, especially if it closes us off to divine energy and guidance arising through the unconscious. Reflecting turn of the century spirituality, Holm's comments sometimes suggest that the physical universe, including the human body, is mere illusion, that material problems, physical symptoms, and psychological disturbances can be overcome through simple denial and affirmation. My view is that reality includes many layers all of which signify or symbolize deeper ones, from superficial to deep, conscious to unconscious, from physiological and psychological to spiritual, from personal and interpersonal to Beyond Personal. In the course of our lives we are called to move from infancy's unconscious oneness to deep conscious individual oneness with God. Along the way life seeks to open us to ever deeper layers of self and reality. Rather than dismissing "bad" circumstances, moods, worries, or symptoms as illusion it is helpful to consider their significance. Rather than condemn, suppress, or repress anger, hurt, fear, envy, sickness as wrong or unreal, ask *to what aspect of myself or of reality is my attention now being called?* I believe even our so-called "bad" feelings, urges, and urgencies are at bottom the surge of God in us. So listen to your feelings, both hurts and heart's desires, in a kindly nonjudgmental way—first *letting up* the feelings, then *letting go of* whatever your well being seems to depend on that is less than God, then *letting go into* God.* A

---

* See the 1997 edition of *Whole Child/Whole Parent* for fuller discussions of this letting up, letting go of, and letting go into approach to prayer and meditation.

loving parent sees through the tantrum of an upset child and asks, "Hey what's up?" Likewise, as you open *The Runner's Bible* ask yourself, "Hey what's up?" Then read and prayerfully consider first what your need is, then how it can be divinely met.

There are many mistaken beliefs of personal and interpersonal power already in the driver's seat of our unawakened psyches, and which can turn life a bumper-car experience. When I go from bed to kitchen to office, from home to town, house to car, family to community, I usually take a moment to check in with *The Runner's Bible*. This helps me to invite God into the driver's seat of my life and to relocate my interpersonal affairs in the larger Beyond Personal spiritual context where God can be counted on to guide, provide, and meet my needs. We do not forget to breathe or imagine that extra breathing in the morning will free us from having to breathe for the rest of the day. Likewise we need to remember to be prayerful throughout the day. As steady breathing provides healthy respiration, frequent prayerful use of *The Runner's Bible* can help us with our ongoing need for inspiration.

I thank Acropolis for making this underground book more widely available, and for allowing me to provide the introduction. Finally, I offer my thanks for Nora Holm and her wonderful *Runner's Bible* which has helped so many of us to run with greater energy, less pounding fear, more love, and a truer sense of direction.

—Polly Berrien Berends

⸻ ••◦◦◉◦◦•• ⸻

Polly Berrien Berends is the author of *Whole Child/Whole Parent, Coming to Life (Traveling the Spiritual Path in Everyday Life),* and *Gently Lead (How to Teach Your Children About God While Finding Out for Yourself).* She is a psychotherapist in Hastings on Hudson, New York.

"IN THE MORNING
WILL I ORDER MY PRAYER
UNTO THEE"

There is nothing as important when making ready for the day, as an early morning period of stillness, wherein to make sure that the Truth, and the Truth only, controls our consciousness. However, that the consciousness may be clear enough to perceive the Truth, we must let go of thoughts and sensations of the material world, must be still (Ps. 46:10) and know that all that truly exists is Good, and determine to know nothing else. This will free from all obstruction the "mind of the flesh" and bring it into harmony with the Mind of the Spirit—with life indeed (Rom. 8:6). We must also be humble (Ps. 37:11), willing to be taught (Prov. 13:18), to receive, and then when joy has been let into the heart (Neh. 8:10), and gratitude is felt, we are in a condition to receive the blessing—to know the Truth, and we can be assured that Love will guide us, that success will ultimately crown every endeavor, for all things will work together for good (Rom. 8:28).

We must also protect ourselves from all that would bring us harm, or even disturb us, by realizing that we are enveloped in an impenetrable armor of love and evil cannot reach us. Our lives are hid with Christ in God (Col. 3:3). We dwell in the secret place of the Most High (Ps. 91:1). His presence shall go with us (Ex. 33:14). So shall we ward off the fiery darts of evil (Eph. 6:15-18), and need not fear what man can do unto us (Heb. 13:6). We shall be safe and can enjoy peace of mind throughout the day. We shall learn, too, that by thus daily seeking the kingdom of God, not only will things be added unto us (Mat. 6:33), but that understanding will rapidly increase because Truth will be more and more revealed.

It will be well to make further preparation for the day by reading verses grouped under the various titles which bear upon our needs, selecting a command to obey and a promise upon which to lean. If we desire the Truth, we will find it here—the Truth which is the remedy for every inharmonious condition. We may not see why, perhaps we cannot, we comprehend so little of spiritual matters; and as practically all of the operations of existence are upon the spiritual plane, it is not wise to refuse to receive assistance because we cannot understand how, nor why it comes. A child may not know why four times four is sixteen, but he learns the fact and uses it—he understands later. We are commanded to become as little children.

THE GODHEAD

God, Christ, Spirit

The Father, the Word, the Holy Ghost.

1 John 5:7.

God—There is none else. Deut. 4:39.

Be not discouraged because you cannot fully comprehend God. For mortal minds this is impossible. But as there is no good apart from Him, you can begin your spiritual life by training yourself to see Him in all good. As He is the only Power, the one Creator, and His work is perfect, so everything must be good, and in everything you will ultimately learn to find Him.

Christ—who hath abolished death, and brought life and immortality to light through the gospel.

2 Tim. 1:10.

Spirit—It is the spirit that quickeneth.

John 6:63.

⌒

All visible life is constantly dependent upon
something besides air—a finer something than
even the air itself. It is the "Fullness of
God"—His Holy Spirit, the Life of Life. In it
"we live and move and have our being."

GOD THE FATHER

I am Alpha and Omega . . . saith the Lord, which is, and which was, and which is to come, the Almighty.
                                                Rev. 1:8.

God is spirit.   John 4:24. (E.R.V.)

Do not I fill heaven and earth? Saith the Lord.
                                                Jer. 23:24.

I am the Lord, and there is none else, there is no God besides me: I girded thee, though thou hast not known me.   Isa. 45:5.

Thou shalt know that I the Lord am thy Savior.
                                                Isa. 60:16.

This is life eternal, that they might know thee, the only true God, and Jesus Christ, whom thou hast sent.   John 17:3.

He that cometh to God must believe that he is.
                                                Heb. 11:6.

Acquaint now thyself with him, and be at peace:
thereby good shall come unto thee.

Job 22:21.

In our desire to understand spiritual existence we must
first reach out after a knowledge of God—to know
Him is to be conscious of eternal life. We must learn
why there can be "none else" than He, and we must try
to comprehend the magnitude of His love and power
that operates unceasingly through His law of good.

Of him, and through him, and to him are all
things.   Rom. 11:36.

There is but one God, the Father, of whom are all
things, and we in him.   1 Cor. 8:6.

For in him we live, and move and have our being.
Acts 17:28.

⮎

He that built all things is God.   Heb. 3:4.

All things were made by him; and without him was
not anything made that was made.   John 1:3.

It is he that hath made us.   Ps. 100:3.

God hath made man upright.   Eccl. 7:29.

Every creature of God is good.   1 Tim. 4:4.

His work is perfect.   Deut. 32:4.

He hath made everything beautiful in its time.
Eccl. 3:11. (E.R.V.)

The earth is full of the goodness of the Lord.
Ps. 33:5.

And God saw everything that he had made, and, behold it was very good.
Gen. 1:31.

Whatsoever God doeth, it shall be forever; nothing can be put to it, nor anything taken from it.
Eccl. 3:14.

If what God created is good and perfect, then evil or imperfection is not from Him. If He made all that was made and finished His work, then evil never was created, and consequently cannot be said to really exist. Evil is indeed a mistaken calculation, an untruth, and must be so considered. One cannot go through life acting upon his own or another's belief that two times two equals five without bringing upon himself and others failure and woe. However, the moment he substitutes a four for the five (truth for the error) the result is correct—is truth. The Truth, in fact, is the universal, scientific remedy for all ills.

Thou hast made heaven, the heaven of heavens, with all their host, the earth, and all things that are therein, the seas, and all that is therein, and thou preservest them all.   Neh. 9:6.

⌒

God is love.   1 John 4:16.

He that dwelleth in love dwelleth in God, and God in him.   1 John 4:16.

Divine Love has one infallible sign, it works good in every way upon all. It does not rob one to bless another, but "in blessing one it blesses all."

For I am persuaded, that neither death, nor life,
nor angels, nor principalities, nor powers, nor
things present, nor things to come, nor height, nor
depth, nor any other creature (creation, E.R.V.),
shall be able to separate us from the love of God,
which is in Christ Jesus our Lord.

Rom. 8:38-39.

☙

The Lord is good. Ps. 100:5.

And Jesus said unto him, Why callest thou me
good? there is none good but one, that is, God.
Mark 10:18.

Thou art good, and doest good. Ps. 119:68.

Thy righteousness is an everlasting righteousness.
Ps. 119:142.

Righteousness and judgment (justice) are the
foundation of his throne. Ps. 97:2. (E.R.V.)

Thy law is the truth. Ps. 119:142.

The law of the Lord is perfect. Ps. 19:7.

Great peace have they which love thy law.
                                        Ps. 119:165.

Open thou mine eyes that I may behold wondrous
things out of thy law.   Ps. 119:18.

Every activity springs from the perpetually active
law of Good.

⌒

The Lord hath made all things for himself.
                                        Prov. 16:4.

All things are thy servants.
                              Ps. 119:91. (E.R.V.)

Each one of us is a divine idea created for a special
purpose, and carrying a distinctive message.

⌒

God is light, and in him is no darkness at all.
                                        1 John 1:5.

In thy light shall we see light.   Ps. 36:9.

There is no power but of God; the powers that be are ordained of God.   Rom. 13:1.

With God all things are possible.

Matt. 19:26.

I am the Lord, the God of all flesh: is there anything too hard for me?   Jer. 32:27.

In the Lord Jehovah is everlasting strength.

Isa. 26:4.

Give up the belief that your strength comes from your brain, nerves and muscles. Your strength comes directly from God. Act upon this law alone.

Thine, oh Lord, is the greatness, and the power, and the glory, and the victory, and the majesty.

1 Chr. 29:11.

Wisdom and might are his.   Dan. 2:20.

Hast thou not known? hast thou not heard? the everlasting God, the Lord, the Creator of the ends of the earth, fainteth not, neither is weary.

Isa. 40:28.

In whom are all the treasures of wisdom, and knowledge hidden. Col. 2:3. (E.R.V.)

O, the depth of the riches both of the wisdom and knowledge of God! how unsearchable are his judgments, and his ways past finding out.

Rom. 11:33.

☙

Thy word is true from the beginning.

Ps. 119:160.

The word of the Lord is living and active.

Heb. 4:12. (E.R.V.)

Man doth not live by bread only, but by every word that proceedeth out of the mouth of the Lord doth man live. Deut. 8:3.

The word of the Lord is right. Ps. 33:4.

The word of the Lord abideth forever.

1 Pet. 1:25. (E.R.V.)

He sendeth his word and healeth them.

Ps. 107:20. (E.R.V.)

For he spake, and it was done. Ps. 33:9.

By the word of the Lord were the heavens made.
Ps. 33:6.

As the rain cometh down, and the snow from heaven, and returneth not thither, but watereth the earth, and maketh it bring forth and bud, that it may give seed to the sower and bread to the eater: so shall my word be that goeth forth out of my mouth; it shall not return unto me void, but it shall accomplish that which I please, and it shall prosper in the thing whereto I sent it.
Isa. 55:10–11.

The words that I speak unto you, they are spirit, and they are life. John 6:63.

Heaven and earth shall pass away; but my words shall not pass away. Luke 21:33.

The sum of thy word is truth.
Ps. 119:160. (E.R.V.)

⌒

I am the Lord, I change not. Mal. 3:6.

The Father of lights, with whom is no variableness, neither shadow of turning.

James 1:17.

Thou art of purer eyes than to behold evil and canst not look on iniquity.   Hab. 1:13.

Unto the pure all things are pure.   Titus 1:15.

God cannot see iniquity any more than a lighted lamp can see darkness. God cannot know evil because evil is a mistake—is untrue. You cannot know that two times two is five, you can only believe it. You can never *know* anything but the truth.

Thou shalt have no other gods before me.

Ex. 20:3.

For all the gods of the peoples are things of nought.

Ps. 96:1. (E.R.V.)

We never fear a person or thing until after we have ascribed power to it, which is to make of it "a god." When you find yourself in fear turn with deep gratitude to the truth that all power comes from the one true God (Rom. 13:1). Firmly deny that this thing which frightens you has any power whatsoever, and you will be free from fear and from danger—freed by the Truth.

Give (ascribe) unto the Lord glory and strength.
Ps. 96:7.

When we look to some person or thing for help we are denying the strength of God, the only real Savior whose word is "living and active," and who is ever ready to help. We are ascribing power to that which has no power—to "things of nought." Heal me and I shall be healed, save me and I shall be saved (Jer. 17:14). Cursed be he that maketh flesh his arm (Jer. 17:5)—who leans from choice upon some material support.

There shall no strange god be in thee. Neither shalt thou worship any strange god. I am the Lord thy God.　　　　　　　　　　　　　　　Ps. 81:9-10.

When we love immoderately material objects, be they our own fleshly bodies, the bodies of our dear ones, or money, or houses, or lands (Mark 10:29), or things we eat, or things we wear, we are having "strange gods" within us.

Shall a man make gods unto himself, and they are no gods?   Jer. 16:20.

Wilt thou set thine eyes upon that which is not? for riches certainly make themselves wings; they fly away as an eagle toward heaven.   Prov. 23:5.

He giveth to all life and breath, and all things.
          Acts 17:25.

We will not think that our life depends upon this material object or that physical action if we know that God is the very source of all life. Our thoughts will not wander after "strange gods" in whom there is no life if we have this understanding.

And it shall be, if thou do at all forget the Lord thy God, and walk after other gods, and serve them, and worship them, I testify against you this day that ye shall surely perish.   Deut. 8:19.

"Blessed is the man whose God is Lord."

They that worship him must worship him in spirit and in truth.   John 4:24.

Make no mental image of divinity. God is spirit and must be spiritually understood. One never gives form nor outline to love, nor to any other spiritual quality. Think of God in limitless terms. Think of Him as universal goodness, an intelligent goodness that is permeated with love, perpetually active and everywhere present (the air is a symbol of that which is everywhere present). Furthermore God is life, all the life we see and know, all the life there is, indestructible and eternal; in fact there is nothing left of reality that is not embraced in God. He is *all* of truth and there is none else (Isa. 45:5). Be assured that if you are satisfied with a mental picture of your Heavenly Father, it is because you do not know Him, "whom to know aright is life eternal."

THE CHRIST OF GOD

I know thee who thou art; the Holy One of God.
                                         Luke 4:34.

⌒

The Word was God.   John 1:1.

The Word was made flesh, and dwelt among us.
                                         John 1:14.

⌒

I am the way, the truth, and the life.   John 14:6.

To this end was I born and for this cause came I
into the world, that I should bear witness unto the
truth.   John 18:37.

Jesus brought the facts of spiritual existence down
to human understanding. Christ revealed through

Jesus the truth about God, man and heaven—that God was universal goodness, that man was inseparably connected with his Father God, and that heaven here upon earth was a condition which resulted from knowing and acknowledging the truths that He taught.

☙

Jesus Christ, the same yesterday, today and forever.
Heb. 13:8.

☙

Christ shall give thee light. Eph. 5:14.

In many places the word truth substituted for the word Christ makes clear the object of Jesus' mission.

☙

Christ is all, and in all. Col. 3:11.

Ye are Christ's; and Christ is God's.
1 Cor. 3:23.

I in them, and thou in me, that they may be perfected into one.   John 17:23. (E.R.V.)

Christ is in and about us always, but we make Him
appear to the spiritually blind, only when we do a
Christ-like act. Whoso gives us a better understanding of life, brings us glad tidings, or even
speaks an encouraging word, is for that moment
the Christ to us—"the Word made flesh"—the
most greatly to be desired accomplishment of
mankind. We should look for Him in every one we
meet, even in the most depraved. He is there, and
encouragement will help to bring Him forth—the
Divine Light—that is to guide us.

⌒

Thou art the Christ, the Son of the living God.
                                          Matt. 16:16.

As many as are led by the Spirit of God, they are
the Sons of God (Rom. 8:14). And if children,
then heirs; heirs of God and joint heirs with Christ
(Rom. 8:17). They which are the children of the
flesh, these are not the children of God (Rom.
9:8).

The Lamb of God which taketh away the sin of the
world.   John 1:29.

He dispels darkness (sin) by the light of Truth and
delivers them who through fear of death were all
their lifetime subject to bondage (Heb. 2:15).

～

Our Savior Jesus Christ, who hath abolished death,
and hath brought life and immortality to light
through the gospel (glad tidings).   2 Tim. 1:10.

Ye call me Teacher, and Lord; and ye say well; for
so I am.   John 13:13. (E.R.V.)

I and the Father are One.
                          John 10:30. (E.R.V.)

Every human being ought to be conscious of this
unity with the Divine One. It is to know the truth
which makes one free.

And all things that are mine are thine, and thine
are mine; and I am glorified in them.
                          John 17:10. (E.R.V.)

He is before all things, and by him all things consist. Col. 1:17.

He is the sustaining Principle of all existence.

In him was life; and the life was the light of men. John 1:4.

I am the light of the world; he that followeth me shall not walk in darkness, but shall have the light of life. John 8:12.

I am the bread of life: he that cometh to me shall never hunger, and he that believeth on me shall never thirst. John 6:35.

Think not that I am come to destroy the law or the prophets: I am not come to destroy, but to fulfil. Matt. 5:17.

I am come that they might have life, and that they might have it more abundantly. John 10:10.

Every one that is of the truth heareth my voice. John 18:37.

Believe in God, believe also in me.

John 14:1. (E.R.V.)

☙

He that abideth in me, and I in him, the same bringeth forth much fruit. John 15:5.

Without me ye can do nothing. John 15:5.

If we calculate without taking into consideration spiritual Truth our calculations come to nought. But if with understanding we apply the law of Truth, our problems will be solved with mathematical exactness and the resulting benefits will be more than we can ask or think.

☙

And he said unto them, Go ye into all the world, and preach the gospel to every creature.

Mark 16:15.

And as ye go, preach, saying, The kingdom of heaven is at hand. Heal the sick, cleanse the lepers, raise the dead, cast out devils: freely ye have received, freely give. Matt. 10:7-8.

For I have given you an example, that ye should do as I have done to you.

John 13:15.

Lo, I am with you always, even unto the end of the world.

Matt. 28:20.

Come unto me all ye that labor and are heavy laden, and I will give you rest. Take my yoke upon you, and learn of me; for I am meek and lowly in heart; and ye shall find rest unto your souls. For my yoke is easy and my burden is light.

Matt. 11:28-30.

To bring your burdens to Christ means to bring them into the light of Truth where their nothingness is revealed and they cease to be burdens. The Truth makes you free of them.

⌒

Peace I leave with you, my peace I give unto you: not as the world giveth, give I unto you. Let not your heart be troubled, neither let it be afraid.

John 14:27.

HIM THAT FILLETH
ALL IN ALL

The Holy Spirit,
The Holy Ghost,
The Spirit of Truth,
The Comforter

Ye shall receive power after that the Holy Ghost is come upon you.

Acts 1:8.

When you first become conscious of the Holy Spirit you will realize that divine power has always been yours.

☞

Howbeit when he, the Spirit of truth, is come, he will guide you into all truth.

John 16:13.

The Comforter (Helper) even the Holy Spirit, whom the Father will send in my name, he shall teach you all things.   John 14:26. (E.R.V.)

～

And I will put my Spirit in you, and ye shall live.
Ezek. 37:14.

I will pour out of my Spirit upon all flesh.
Acts. 2:17.

It has always been "upon" you, around you and through you. From it you have drawn, though unconsciously, all the power that you have used in your senses, your intellect, in every way (Isa. 45:5). But your eyes have been closed and you have not seen the greater possibilities. In the midst of plenty—enough for every need, every aim—you have not had sufficient understanding to open your eyes and take possession. Finally something awakens you—it is often sorrow—and then you see the Truth, that this, in which you live, move, and have your being, is the seat of all Power, "the very present Help," the inexhaustible treasury of Good. Then you hasten to put yourself in harmony with it by right thinking, humility and faith.

Know ye not that ye are the temple of God, and that the Spirit of God dwelleth in you?

1 Cor. 3:16.

There is a friend that sticketh closer than a brother.   Prov. 18:24.

It is God which worketh in you both to will and to do of his good pleasure.

Phil. 3:13.

(Ye) are built upon the foundation of the apostles and prophets, Jesus Christ himself being the chief cornerstone; in whom all the building fitly framed together groweth unto a holy temple in the Lord: In whom ye also are builded together for a habitation of God through the Spirit.

Eph. 2:20-22.

Where the Spirit of the Lord is, there is liberty.

2 Cor. 3:17.

And hereby we know that he abideth in us, by the Spirit which he hath given us.

1 John 3:24.

I have put my words in thy mouth.   Isa. 51:16.

It is not ye that speak, but the Spirit of your Father which speaketh in you.

Matt. 10:20.

It is the Spirit that beareth witness, because the Spirit is the truth.   1 John 5:7.

The testimony of the material senses is false. Silence it by the Truth.

☙

For the Holy Spirit shall teach you in that very hour what ye ought to say.

Luke 12:12. (E.R.V.)

Not by might, nor by power, but by my Spirit, saith the Lord of hosts.   Zech. 4:6.

For no prophecy ever came by the will of man: but men spake from God, being moved by the Holy Ghost.   2 Pet. 1:21.

And they were all filled with the Holy Spirit and began to speak with other tongues, as the Spirit gave them utterance.   Acts 2:4. (E.R.V.)

It is the spirit that quickeneth (that giveth life), the flesh profiteth nothing: the words that I speak unto you, they are spirit, and they are life.

John 6:63.

The thoughts that spring up within us as we gain an understanding of Christ's words of truth, make us anew in mind, to become finally manifest as health, vigor and comeliness of body.

Likewise, the Spirit also helpeth our infirmities.

Rom. 8:26.

But if the Spirit of him that raised up Jesus from the dead dwell in you, he that raised up Christ from the dead shall also quicken (give life to) your mortal bodies by his Spirit that dwelleth in you.

Rom. 8:11.

⮞

Behold, I give unto you power to tread on serpents and scorpions, and over all the power of the enemy; and nothing shall by any means hurt you.

Luke 10:19.

And the seventy returned again with joy, saying, Lord, even the devils are subject unto us through thy name.   Luke 10:17.

That good thing which was committed unto thee guard through the Holy Ghost which dwelleth in us.   2 Tim. 1:14.

Ye have an anointing from the Holy One, and ye know all things.   1 John 2:20. (E.R.V.)

The fruit of the Spirit is love, joy, peace, long-suffering, gentleness, goodness, faith.

Gal. 5:22.

For this commandment which I command thee this day, it is not too hard for thee, neither is it far off. It is not in heaven, that thou shouldst say, Who shall go up for us to heaven, and bring it unto us, and make us to hear it, that we may do it? Neither is it beyond the sea, that thou shouldst say, who shall go over the sea for us, and bring it unto us, and make us to hear it, that we may do it? But the word is very nigh unto thee, in thy mouth, and in thy heart, that thou mayest do it.

Deut. 30:11-14. (E.R.V.)

Now we have received, not the spirit of the world, but the spirit which is of God; that we might know the things that are freely given to us of God.

1 Cor. 2:12.

HIS IMAGE AND LIKENESS

God created man in his own image. In the image of
God created he him. Gen. 1:27

Man is the child of God. He is upright (Eccl.
7:29), good (1 John 3:9-10, Gen. 1:31), beautiful
(Eccl. 3:11), perfect (Deut. 32:4), spiritual (Job
33:4), and eternal (Eccl. 3:14), the image and
likeness of his Creator. Authority is granted to him
over himself and everything else (last clause Isa.
45:11; Ps. 8:6-8; Heb. 2:7-8) and he becomes a
responsible being, accountable to God. He has
explicit directions (Prov. 6:23), and everything
needful is divinely assured him (Phil. 4:19) to help
him to express the Perfect Life—everything except
desire and faith, these must come from him and
these he *must use*. Visible man, the sick and sinning
mortal, is one whose first and greatest desire was to
play awhile with the things of the material world.
Becoming absorbed in the game, his real life and
its belongings have been forgotten, and the belief

has possession of him that the game and the play-things are all there is to life. The result of this false belief is a decaying, dying body of flesh, stinging with desires that destroy. Often mortal man grows tired of this which he calls "Life," for pain follows closer and closer upon the heels of each pleasure, and nothing is left that satisfies. He is sick, disappointed, forsaken, and he envies the swine their food. He wishes to die. Often out of the depths of such misery comes a cry for help. Truth answers and calls the man by his right name, assuring him that this experience which he has just been through is not real, it is but the game that he has been playing: that his belief in it and his devotion to it have caused all of his woe. This brings the wretched man to himself, and he acknowledges that he had forgotten his real life, his home, his God; he had forgotten that he was a child of God and as such could have had all the help that he needed. Then he quickly arises in his thoughts, and goes to his Father's house where there is enough and to spare, where all is Love and where happiness unspeakable is everlasting (Luke 15:18). Thus by changing his belief and his habit of thought, his "mind is renewed," and through that he becomes "transformed" (Rom. 8:13), old things pass away, all things become new. The true replaces the false, the evidences of the game and the results of his false belief vanish (Isa. 1:18), his visible body is once more pure and healthy; and his mind is at rest, for he finds himself in the arms of his loving Father, the unchanging God, the Ruler of all, where nothing can harm him or make him afraid, and where all is peace and joy forever.

We know that whosoever is born of God sinneth not; but he that is begotten of God keepeth himself, and that wicked one toucheth him not.

1 John 5:18.

☞

He that is joined unto the Lord is one spirit.

1 Cor. 6:17.

The real spiritual man's relation to his Father, God, is much the same as that of the sunbeam to the sun. Nothing can separate from the sun any one of its rays. Made of its substance, partaking of its nature—its image and likeness—the sun gives to each a particular mission, a certain angle to fill with its light and heat. Man is God's offspring

(Acts 17:29), coexists with Him, is eternal. Connected with the Source of supply nothing can prevent all that he needs from being his, life, breath and all things. Like the sunbeam each man has his own angle to fill, his special work to do; and in order that he may have all possible assistance God has given him dominion over everything—everything except his brother man. Thus each individual is a part of the divine plan necessary to the perfect whole.

All mine are thine, and thine are mine.

John 17:10.

"One with God is a majority."

Thou madest him a little lower than the angels; thou crownedst him with glory and honor, and didst set him over the works of thy hands: Thou hast put all things in subjection under his feet. For in that he put all in subjection under him, he left nothing that is not put under him. But now we see not yet all things put under him.

Heb. 2:7-8.

The Spirit of God hath made me, and the breath of the Almighty giveth me life.

Job 33:4.

(I) shall put my spirit in you, and ye shall live, and I will place you in your own land.

Ezek. 37:14.

I will put my Spirit within you, and cause you to walk in my statutes, and ye shall keep my judgments, and do them.   Ezek. 36:27.

I have filled him with the Spirit of God, in wisdom, and in understanding, and in knowledge, and in all manner of workmanship.   Ex. 31:3.

Man doth not live by bread only, but by every word that proceedeth out of the mouth of the Lord doth man live.   Deut. 8:3.

If ye live after the flesh, ye must die: but if by the spirit ye make to die the deeds of the body, ye shall live.   Rom. 8:13. (E.R.V.)

He that loseth his life (his physical sense of life) for my sake (because it is not the truth and the truth is what he wants), shall find it (Matt. 10:39). I (Truth) am come that they might have life, and that they might have it more abundantly. (John 10:10). Examine yourself to see if you are willing to give up all of your old beliefs for the incoming of a higher ideal of life—"the life more abundant."

I am persuaded, that neither death nor life, nor principalities, nor powers, nor things present, nor things to come, nor height, nor depth, nor any other creatures shall be able to separate us from the love of God, which is in Christ Jesus our Lord.

Rom. 8:38-39.

WALK IN LOVE

And one of the scribes came and heard them questioning together, and knowing that he had answered them well, asked him, What commandment is the first of all? Jesus answered, The first is, Hear O Israel; The Lord our God, the Lord is one: and thou shalt love the Lord thy God from all thy heart, and from all thy soul, and from all thy mind, and from all thy strength. The second is this, Thou shalt love thy neighbor as thyself. There is none other commandment greater than these. And the scribe said unto him, Of a truth, Teacher, thou hast well said that he is one; and there is none other but he: and to love him with all the heart, and with all the understanding, and with all the strength, and to love his neighbor as himself is much more than all whole burnt offerings and sacrifices.

Mark 12:28-33. (E.R.V.)
(Read also Matt. 22:34-40 and Luke 10:25-37.)

Ever feel an outgoing of love from the very best that is within you to your Father, God. Love Him as you do your life, for He is your life. Keep yourself constantly in His love (Jude 21) by loving others as yourself, for He is their Life as well as yours, and by maintaining a loving attitude toward life in general, for Life is God and "God is Love."

God is love.   1 John 4:16.

It will help your understanding to substitute the word Love for the word God in many scriptural passages. Love is a synonym for God.

God (Love) is my strength and power.
                                                    2 Sam. 22:33.

To love is to have power, and to be loved is to be given more power.

Let all that ye do be done in love.
                                            1 Cor. 16:14. (E.R.V.)

Be sure that there is nothing but love in your thoughts for God, for man, and for your work before you begin any special task. This is to put

God into it, which means power for the execution and perfection in the result, that is if Love is entirely your master.

Love is the motive power behind all divine activity.

All things were made by him (God, Love).

John 1:3.

Love is the only creative power. It flows from God to man, and man recognizing it accomplishes what seems to be humanly impossible.

There is no power but of God (Love).

Rom. 13:1.

If some difficulty presents itself, become filled with a realization of the power of Love. Then be patient and see how Love saves (Deut. 20:4). It "shall fight for you and ye shall hold your peace" (Ex. 14:14). Love being the activity of God it is that which actually does the work. It is the only Power, and when we do not interfere it saves us.

Walk in love.   Eph. 5:2.
Be active in love.

He that dwelleth in love dwelleth in God.

1 John 4:16.

Thou shalt love thy neighbor as thyself.

Lev. 19:18.

If ye fulfil the royal law according to the Scripture,
Thou shalt love thy neighbor as thyself, ye do well.

James 2:8.

This is the message that ye heard from the beginning, that we should love one another.

1 John 3:11.

See that ye love one another with a pure heart fervently. 1 Pet. 1:22.

He that despiseth his neighbor is void of wisdom.

Prov. 11:12. (E.R.V.)

Above all things being fervent in your love among yourselves; for love covereth a multitude of sins.

1 Pet. 4:8. (E.R.V.)

Owe no man anything, but to love one another, for he that loveth another hath fulfilled the law. Love

worketh no ill to his neighbor; therefore love is the
fulfilling of the law.

Rom. 13:8, 10.

Beloved, let us love one another; for love is of
God; and everyone that loveth is born of God, and
knoweth God. He that loveth not knoweth not
God; for God is love.

1 John 4:7-8.

He that saith he is in the light, and hateth his
brother, is in darkness even until now. He that
loveth his brother abideth in the light and there is
none occasion of stumbling in him. But he that
hateth his brother is in darkness and walketh in
darkness and knoweth not whither he goeth, because that darkness hath blinded his eyes.

1 John 2:9-11.

Hate in the thoughts generates a deadly poison in
the body which kills if it is not neutralized by love.
All they that hate me love death (Prov. 8:36).
Where hate is there can be no health, no success,
no happiness. Hate works evil only to him who
hates. It is the thickest of all veils that hide our
blessings. Where envy and strife (forms of hate)

are, there is confusion and every evil thing (James 3:16, E.R.V.).

We know that we have passed from death unto life because we love the brethren.

1 John 3:14.

Love is an awakener, it brings forth life, it renews the body by changing thoughts of death unto thoughts of life. He that loveth not abideth in death (1 John 3:14, E.R.V.).

Through love be servants one to another.

Gal. 5:13. (E.R.V.)

If we serve others through love we serve ourselves as well.

Love ye therefore the stranger: for ye were strangers in the land of Egypt.

Deut. 10:19.

But the stranger that dwelleth with you shall be unto you as one born among you, and thou shalt love him as thyself.　　　　Lev. 19:34.

Love is understood by everything that breathes. It is the universal language. It is the sign of God.

But I say unto you which hear, Love your enemies, do good to them which hate you. Bless them that curse you, and pray for them which despitefully use you.

Luke 6:27-28.

Have we not all one Father? Hath not one God created us?   Mal. 2:10.

When you meet another, no matter what his station in life, his creed or color, let this thought go through you: His life and my life are one, one love sustains us both (Acts 10:28).

☞

Let all that ye do be done in love.

1 Cor. 16:14. (E.R.V.)

And above all these things put on love, which is the bond of perfectness.

Col. 3:14. (E.R.V.)

No man hath seen God at any time. If we love one another, God dwelleth in us, and his love is perfected in us. 1 John 4:12.

We cannot see God any more than we can see love. But we recognize Him in loving kindness.

By this shall all men know that ye are my disciples, if ye have love one to another.

John 13:35.

Knowledge puffeth up, but love buildeth up.
1 Cor. 8:1. (E.R.V.)

Hatred stirreth up strifes; but love covereth all sins.
Prov. 10:12.

If a brother has in penitence cast aside sin you will speed him into happiness by veiling his past from the world with your own loving silence.

No one deserving the name of Christian ever resurrects another's sinful past to his shame.

Let all bitterness, and wrath, and anger, and clamor, and evil speaking, be put away from you, with all malice. Eph. 4:31.

The wrath of man worketh not the righteousness of God. James 1:20.

⸏

If I speak with the tongues of men and of angels, but have not love, I am become sounding brass, or a clanging cymbal. And if I have the gift of prophecy, and know all mysteries and all knowledge, and if I have all faith, so as to remove mountains, but have not love, I am nothing. And if I bestow all my goods to feed the poor, and if I give my body to be burned, but have not love, it profiteth me nothing. Love suffereth long, and is kind; love envieth not; love vaunteth not itself; is not puffed up, doth not behave itself unseemly, seeketh not its own, is not provoked, taketh not account of evil; rejoiceth not in unrighteousness, but rejoiceth with the truth; beareth all things, believeth all things, hopeth all things, endureth all things. Love never faileth; but whether there be prophecies, they shall be done away; whether there be tongues, they shall cease; whether there be knowledge, it shall be done away. For we know in part, and we prophecy in part; but when that which is perfect is come, that which is in part shall be done away. 1 Cor. 13:1-10. (E.R.V.)

Love not the world, neither the things that are in the world. If any man love the world, the love of the Father is not in him. For all that is in the world, the lust of the flesh and the lust of the eyes and the pride of life, is not of the Father, but is of the world. And the world passeth away and the lust thereof; but he that doeth the will of God abideth forever.

1 John 2:15-17.

⌒

But the end of the charge is love out of a pure heart and a good conscience and faith unfeigned.

1 Tim. 1:5. (E.R.V.)

REJOICE ALWAYS

There is no command of greater importance given in the Bible, nor one more often repeated, nor less heeded than this command to rejoice. When man rejoices in that which is good he is lifted, whether he knows it or not, into his highest consciousness—into his true Self, where divine Light dispels the darkness of sin and sickness. You have noticed that the happy man is usually healthy and fortunate. The world says he is happy because he is healthy and fortunate; but the truth is he is healthy and fortunate because he is happy, because a spiritual law is obeyed. All things gravitate to those who keep the commandments. Fear and sorrow are enemies of man; they begin by tearing down the material body, they end in death. Joy is of Heaven.

Rejoice in the Lord, O ye righteous; for praise is comely for the upright.   Ps. 33:1.

Be glad in the Lord, and rejoice, ye righteous; and shout for joy, all ye that are upright in heart.

Ps. 32:11.

Praise ye the Lord. Praise ye the Lord from the heavens. Praise him in the heights.

Ps. 148:1.

I will bless the Lord at all times; his praise shall continually be in my mouth.

Ps. 34:1.

One way of praising God is to praise the good whenever and wherever you find it.

⌒

Be ye glad and rejoice forever in that which I create.   Isa. 65:18.

For every creature of God is good, and nothing is to be rejected if it be received with thanksgiving: for it is sanctified through the word of God and prayer.

1 Tim. 4:4-5. (E.R.V.)

For thou Lord, hast made me glad through thy work; I will triumph in the works of thy hands.

Ps. 92:4.

Thou shalt rejoice in every good thing which the Lord thy God hath given unto thee, and unto thine house. Deut. 26:11.

Go thy way, eat thy bread with joy. Eccl. 9:7.

Joy is both an appetizer and a digester, it should flavor all that we eat. Never discuss unpleasant subjects at the table.

⌒

The Lord thy God shall bless thee in all thy increase, and in all the works of thine hands, therefore thou shalt surely rejoice. Deut. 16:15.

Ye shall rejoice in all that ye put your hand unto.

Deut. 12:7.

To rejoice calls into action divine power, and if he who rejoices have both faith and understanding, success is assured.

Delight thyself also in the Lord, and he shall give thee the desires of thine heart.

Ps. 37:4.

Let the people praise thee, O God; let all the people praise thee. Then shall the earth yield her increase and God even our own God shall bless us.

Ps. 67:5-6.

Wherefore I perceive that there is nothing better than that a man should rejoice in his works; for that is his portion.   Eccl. 3:22.

I know that there is nothing better for them than to rejoice, and to do good so long as they live.

Eccl. 3:12. (E.R.V.)

☙

The joy of the Lord is your strength.

Neh. 8:10.

Cultivate happiness, endeavor to *look* pleasant. No matter what your mood, act always as though you were happy. Happiness is contagious and it is every Christian's duty to add to this world's store of it.

For the kingdom of God is not eating and drinking, but righteousness and peace, and joy in the Holy Ghost. Rom. 14:17.

One of the fruits of the Spirit is "joy" (Gal. 5:22).

☞

Lo, this is our God; we have waited for him, and he will save us; this is the Lord; we have waited for him, and we will be glad and rejoice in his salvation. Isa. 25:9.

The Lord is my strength and my shield; my heart trusted in him, and I am helped; therefore my heart greatly rejoiceth; and with my song will I praise him. Ps. 28:7.

I have set the Lord always before me; because he is at my right hand, I shall not be moved. Therefore my heart is glad, and my glory rejoiceth; my flesh also shall dwell in safety.

Ps. 16:8-9. (E.R.V.)

For ye shall go out with joy, and be led forth with peace; the mountains and the hills shall break forth before you into singing, and all the trees of the field shall clap their hands. Instead of the thorn shall come up the fir tree; and instead of the briar shall come up the myrtle tree.

Isa. 55:12-13.

The wilderness and the parched land shall be glad; and the desert shall rejoice, and blossom as the rose.   Isa. 35:1. (E.R.V.)

The pastures are clothed with flocks; the valleys also are covered over with corn; They shout for joy, they also sing.   Ps. 65:13.

Thou makest the outgoings of the morning and evening to rejoice.   Ps. 65:8.

The ransomed of Jehovah shall return, and come with singing unto Zion: and everlasting joy shall be upon their heads: they shall obtain gladness and joy; and sorrow and sighing shall flee away.

Isa. 51:11.

Oh, that men would praise the Lord for his goodness and for his wonderful works to the children of men.   Ps. 107:8.

IN EVERYTHING
GIVE THANKS

Be ye thankful. Col. 3:15.

Begin to give thanks even before you open your eyes in the morning. As consciousness creeps over you, follow it with a thankful prayer for life, that a new day, another chance is yours—and be glad in your heart of hearts that you have faith in God, and at least a partial understanding of divine law. Be thankful for the beauty of the morning, that you have eyes to see it and the faculty to enjoy it, and as the day advances, forget not to be grateful over the small joys as well as the large ones—the new flower, the book, the letter, the meeting with friends, the kindly word; be thankful for knowledge, for the lessons that come through mistakes and misfortune; be glad that the misfortune is no worse; in fact be thankful for everything; for as one who recognizes his union with Divinity, you know that only good comes to you.

The least you must give is a thankful heart, and a thankful heart is a fertile field; the Lord plants the seeds of his richest blessings in just such a field.

⌒

Continue steadfastly in prayer; watching therein with thanksgiving.

Col. 4:2. (E.R.V.)

Giving thanks always for all things in the name of our Lord Jesus Christ to God, even the Father.

Eph. 5:20. (E.R.V.)

⌒

Praise ye the Lord. O give thanks unto the Lord; for his is good; for his mercy endureth forever.

Ps. 106:1.

Be deeply grateful for the divine law of God—that it is ever active, ever present, unchanging and eternal.

Offer unto God thanksgiving; and pay thy vows unto the Most High. And call upon me in the day

of trouble; I will deliver thee, and thou shalt glorify
me.

Ps. 50:14-15.

And one of them, when he saw that he was healed,
turned back, with a loud voice glorifying God; and
he fell down upon his face at his feet, giving him
thanks, and he was a Samaritan. And Jesus answering said, Were not the ten cleansed? but where are
the nine? Were there none found that returned to
give glory to God, save this stranger?

Luke 17:15-18. (E.R.V.)

The world—and that includes those who call
themselves Christians—seems sadly lacking in
gratitude. Even when it is felt, some are unwilling
to humble themselves enough to express it; or what
is worse they are reluctant to give pleasure by such
expression. Thanks, sincerely and humbly given,
may be just the encouragement the recipient
needs—true, spiritual food. At least it will let in a
little of God's sunshine upon a very dark world.

Gratitude is the most active healing agent so-called
mortal man can employ. Too much emphasis
cannot be placed upon the command to give
thanks.

O give thanks unto the Lord; call upon his name; make known his deeds among the people. Sing unto him, sing psalms unto him; talk ye of all his wondrous works. Glory ye in his holy name; let the heart of them rejoice that seek the Lord.

Ps. 105:1-3.

My meditation of him shall be sweet: I will be glad in the Lord. Ps. 104:34.

Many, O Lord my God, are thy wonderful works which thou hast done, and thy thoughts which are to us-ward: they cannot be reckoned up in order unto thee; if I would declare and speak of them, they are more than can be numbered.

Ps. 40:5.

Let us come before his presence with thanksgiving.

Ps. 95:2.

Enter into his gates with thanksgiving, and into his courts with praise. Give thanks unto him, and bless his name. For the Lord is good: his mercy endureth forever: and his faithfulness unto all generations.

Ps. 100:4.

Blessed be the Lord, that hath given rest unto his people Israel, according to all that he promised: there hath not failed one word of all his good promise, which he promised by the hand of Moses, his servant.   Kings 8:56.

Thanks be to God for his unspeakable gift.
                                    2 Cor. 9:15.

Thanks be to God who giveth us the victory through our Lord Jesus Christ.
                                    1 Cor. 15:57.

O that men would praise the Lord for his goodness, and for his wonderful works to the children of men.   Ps. 107:8.

I will sing unto the Lord, because he hath dealt bountifully with me.
                                    Ps. 13:6. (E.R.V.)

In all thy ways acknowledge him and he will make plain thy paths.
                                    Prov. 3:6. (E.R.V.)

The ever grateful heart is in harmony with the activity of Good, and its needs are always supplied.

The remark is often heard concerning those in perpetual want, "You need not expect gratitude from that class;" the truth is "that class" is composed of the habitually unthankful, who, ignoring a divine law, are adrift and ever in want.

⮜

It is a good thing to give thanks unto the Lord, and to sing praises unto thy name, O Most High: to show forth thy lovingkindness in the morning, and thy faithfulness every night.

Ps. 92:1-2.

⮜

Let everything that hath breath praise the Lord. Praise ye the Lord.   Ps. 150:6.

FEAR NOT, ONLY BELIEVE

Let not your heart be troubled; believe in God,
believe also in me.

John 14:1. (E.R.V.)

With God all things are possible.

Matt. 19:26.

Without Him nothing is certain. Useless toil,
confusion, loss of way, discouragement, sickness
are apt to mean failure to one who works without
God in his consciousness.

Believe in the Lord your God, so shall ye be established; believe his prophets, so shall ye prosper.

2 Chr. 20:20.

Whatsoever is not of faith, is sin.

Rom. 14:23.

Without faith it is impossible to please him; for he that cometh to God must believe that he is.

Heb. 11:6.

Have faith in God. Mark 11:22.

Fear not; for I am with thee. Isa. 43:5.

I will not fail thee, nor forsake thee. Josh. 1:5.

Trust in the Lord with all thine heart; and lean not unto thine own understanding.

Prov. 3:5.

The wisdom of this world is foolishness with God.

1 Cor. 3:19.

⌐

Commit thy way unto the Lord; trust also in him, and he shall bring it to pass.

Ps. 37:5.

Be not therefore anxious for the morrow; for the morrow will be anxious for itself. Sufficient unto the day is the evil thereof. Matt. 6:34. (E.R.V.)

No true believer ever worries; to worry is to insult your God.

He that trusteth in his own heart is a fool.

Prov. 28:26.

Wait for Jehovah; be strong, and let thy heart take courage; yea, wait thou for Jehovah.

Ps. 27:14.

The righteous shall live by faith.

Rom. 1:17. (E.R.V.)

And all things whatsoever ye shall ask in prayer, believing, ye shall receive.　　　Matt. 21:22.

Therefore I say unto you, what things soever ye desire, when ye pray, believe that ye receive them, and ye shall have them.　　　Mark 11:24.

Believe the truth that Good is ever unfolding for you and it will become a visible possession.

And Jesus said unto him, if thou canst believe, all things are possible to him that believeth.

Mark 9:23.

The fear of man bringeth a snare; but whoso putteth his trust in the Lord shall be safe.

Prov. 29:25.

Preserve my life from fear of the enemy (Ps. 64:1). Put fear behind you out of sight and mind, rebuke it as you do other sins—it is one of the worst of them. "The enemy" may be a human foe, a bad habit, a false belief, or any peace destroyer.

Some trust in chariots, and some in horses; but we will make mention of the name of Jehovah our God.

Ps. 20:7. (E.R.V.)

For ye have not received the spirit of bondage again to fear.

Rom. 8:15.

There is no fear in love; but perfect love casteth out fear; because fear hath punishment, and he that feareth is not made perfect in love.

1 John 4:18. (E.R.V.)

One fears because one does not fully realize that there is no power in anything but good—but God, and God is Love, and "Love worketh no ill." We lose fear in proportion as we gain an understanding of God. (Read also Isa. 51:12-16).

He shall not be afraid of evil tidings; his heart is fixed, trusting in the Lord. Ps. 112:7.

The fear of the wicked, it shall come upon him; but the desire of the righteous shall be granted.

Prov. 10:24.

As for God, his way is perfect; the word of the Lord is tried; he is a shield unto all them that take refuge in him.

2 Sam. 22:31. (E.R.V.)

Through faith we understand that the worlds were framed by the word of God, so that things which are seen were not made of things which do appear.

Heb. 11:3.

The apostles said unto the Lord, Increase our faith. And the Lord said, If ye had faith as a grain of mustard seed, ye might say unto this sycamine tree, Be thou plucked up by the root, and be thou planted in the sea: and it should obey you.

Luke 17:5-6.

For verily I say unto you, that whosoever shall say unto this mountain, Be thou removed, and be thou cast into the sea; and shall not doubt in his heart, but shall believe that those things which he saith shall come to pass, he shall have whatsoever he saith.   Mark 11:23.

If this be a mountain of fear, of remorse, of worry, of hurtful habits, of ill health, of anything that like a mountain obscures from our view the land of peace and happiness, one word of command—if there be faith—and the mountain is removed and cast into oblivion.

And these signs shall follow them that believe: in my name shall they cast out demons; they shall speak with new tongues; they shall take up serpents, and if they drink any deadly thing, it shall in no wise hurt them; they shall lay hands on the sick, and they shall recover.

Mark 16:17-18.

He that giveth heed unto the word shall find good; and whoso trusteth in the Lord, happy is he.

Prov. 16:20.

He that trusteth in his riches shall fall: but the righteous shall flourish as a branch.

Prov. 11:28.

⌒

I had fainted, unless I had believed to see the goodness of the Lord in the land of the living.

Ps. 27:13.

And the Lord helpeth them, and rescueth them; he rescueth them from the wicked, and saveth them, because they have taken refuge in him.

Ps. 37:40.

When thou goest forth to battle against thine enemies, and seest horses, and chariots, and a people more than thou, thou shalt not be afraid of them; for the Lord thy God is with thee. For the Lord your God is he that goeth with you, to fight for you against your enemies, to save you.

Deut. 20:1, 4. (E.R.V.)

The Lord is my light and my salvation; whom shall I fear? The Lord is the strength of my life; of whom shall I be afraid?

Ps. 27:1.

Blessed is the man that trusteth in the Lord, and whose trust the Lord is. For he shall be as a tree planted by the waters, that spreadeth out its roots by the river, and shall not fear when heat cometh, but its leaf shall be green; and shall not be careful in the year of drought, neither shall cease from yielding fruit.

Jer. 17:7-8. (E.R.V.)

Cursed is the man that trusteth in man, and maketh flesh his arm, and whose heart departeth from the Lord. For he shall be like the heath in the desert, and shall not see when good cometh, but shall inhabit the parched places in the wilderness, a salt land and not inhabited.

Jer. 17:5-6. (E.R.V.)

⌐

The just shall live by his faith.   Hab. 2:4.

Happy is he that hath the God of Jacob for his help, whose hope is in the Lord his God.

Ps. 146:5.

Thy faith hath saved thee; go in peace.

Luke 7:50.

GET WISDOM, GET UNDERSTANDING

Ye shall know the truth, and the truth shall make you free.   John 8:32.

Evil is not true. It is but a belief that the untrue is true; and this belief fastens itself upon the consciousness of man and controls his thoughts and actions to his harm. Evil is one universal mistake, just as the belief that the earth was square was a universal mistake, that kept men stumbling in its darkness until one came holding aloft the light of his divine message. The darkness disappeared with the coming of this light, the evil vanished for it was only a belief—with the coming in of the Truth.

The wisdom that is from above is first pure, then peaceable, gentle, easy to be entreated, full of mercy and good fruits, without doubtfulness, without hypocrisy.   James 3:17. (E.R.V.)

For to the man that pleaseth him God giveth
wisdom, and knowledge, and joy.

Eccl. 2:26. (E.R.V.)

But to the sinner he giveth travail, to gather and to
heap up, that he may give him that is good before
God.   Eccl. 2:26.

The man who ignores Divine Law *may chance* to
heap up wealth without hard work, but lacking
spiritual understanding he will not be able to make
it add to his happiness; and very likely he will at
last discover that he has been a tool in the Almighty's hand to bring the blessing of abundance to
those who keep the commandments and govern the
material things that they use through spiritual
understanding.

Call unto me, and I will answer thee, and show thee
great and mighty things which thou knowest not.

Jer. 33:3.

Cultivate a desire to know the things of the Spirit,
make the getting of wisdom a passion; welcome
each new thought as though it were the first that
you had ever received; try to find a lesson in every

experience, expect a message from each one you meet, make an effort to see from the other's point of view; *and be meek*—meekness is the only soil in which spiritual knowledge will grow.

⌐

The meek will he guide in judgment: and the meek will he teach his way.   Ps. 25:9.

Receive with meekness the engrafted word, which is able to save your souls.

James 1:21.

⌐

But ask now the beasts, and they shall teach thee; and the fowls of the air, and they shall tell thee; or speak to the earth, and it shall teach thee; and the fishes of the sea shall declare unto thee.

Job 12:7.

Search for the spiritual meaning of everything. Think of things as symbols. The air is symbolic of the fullness of God, His Holy Spirit that gives Life and Power to all things; the sunshine typifies His joy-dispensing Love; the rain that falls upon the just and the unjust, His loving care; the depths of the ocean, or the valleys between the hills suggest Peace; the rose speaks Beauty, and the radiant sunsets, the Glory that we've found in our new life—the Life of the Spirit. Thus little by little hidden meanings will be revealed and the wisdom of God be made more clearly manifest.

Take fast hold of instruction; let her not go; keep her; for she is thy life.   Prov. 4:13.

Blessed are the meek: for they shall inherit the earth.   Matt. 5:5.

Put on therefore . . . humbleness of mind.
                                                Col. 3:12.

Before honor is humility.   Prov. 15:33.

It is of utmost importance to possess humility. It means that one is receptive, teachable; growth and achievement follow naturally. Without humility the world lags, even retrogrades. The lack of this divine attribute accounts for the commonplaceness of the world in general. One who hugs his precious opinions to himself clips his own wings. The great ones of earth are humble. Greatness though knocks at every door, but the door is usually barred and double barred by old beliefs, pride of opinion, or selfish contentment. Real humility values nothing as it does the Truth, and is ever ready to receive it.

The reward of humility and the fear of the Lord is riches, and honor and life.

Prov. 22:4. (E.R.V.)

A scorner seeketh wisdom, and findeth it not.

Prov. 14:6.

The scorner has blinded his own eyes. The doubter neutralizes the power of all knowledge that comes to him.

Let no man deceive himself. If any man thinketh that he is wise among you in this world, let him become a fool that he may become wise.

1 Cor. 3:18.

Be teachable. Do not allow self-conceit to shut the door in Wisdom's face. Much of our knowledge is little better than a cobweb, it needs to be swept away. Pride of intellect is an enemy that prevents Truth from coming to us. Do not try to force new ideas to coincide with old ones.

Thus saith the Lord, Let not the wise man glory in his wisdom, neither let the mighty man glory in his might, let not the rich man glory in his riches: but let him that glorieth glory in this, that he understandeth and knoweth me, that I am the Lord which exercise lovingkindness, judgment, and righteousness, in the earth: for in these things I delight, saith the Lord.   Jer. 9:23-24.

Faith by being permeated with understanding is given an active quality which it does not possess when standing alone. Oxygen gives activity to the air. The dynamo produces electricity which moves things. Understanding with faith moves things, works. Faith without understanding is incomplete in its accomplishment.

Walk with wise men and thou shalt be wise.
                                        Prov. 13:20.

Make no friendship with an angry man; and with a furious man thou shalt not go: lest thou learn his ways, and get a snare to thy soul.

Prov. 22:24-25.

Wherefore, my beloved brethren, let every man be swift to hear, slow to speak, slow to wrath: For the wrath of man worketh not the righteousness of God.

James 1:19-20.

⌒

He that keepeth understanding shall find good.

Prov. 19:8.

Self-pity must be strangled the moment it is recognized. It is the worm that dieth not. To indulge in self-pity is to tear down your own strongholds. If you have spiritual understanding even in a small degree, you will know that continued misfortune indicates that something is clouding your consciousness of Ever-Present Help, you are engaged in wrongdoing, are holding to the belief that some act of the past has power to harm you, are indulging in some form of hate, or you are not protecting yourself as you should "from the fiery darts of evil." Self-pity has no place in the divine economy, and should be reckoned with worry and regret as agents of death. No cure can come, nor inharmony be banished, while any one of these three has control of the thoughts.

The mouth of the righteous speaketh wisdom.

Ps. 37:30.

Get wisdom, get understanding: forget it not; neither decline from the words of my mouth. Forsake her not, and she shall preserve thee: love her, and she shall keep thee. Wisdom is the principal thing; therefore get wisdom: and with all thy getting get understanding. Exalt her, and she shall promote thee: she shall bring thee to honor, when thou dost embrace her. She shall give to thine head an ornament of grace: a crown of glory shall she deliver to thee. Prov. 4:5-9.

Brethren, be not children in understanding: howbeit in malice be ye children, but in understanding be men. 1 Cor. 14:20.

Wherefore be ye not foolish, but understand what the will of the Lord is.

Eph. 5:17. (E.R.V.)

Turn you at my reproof, behold, I will pour out my spirit unto you, I will make known my words unto you.   Prov. 1:23.

Man that is in honor and understandeth not, is like the beasts that perish.   Ps. 49:20.

If any of you lacketh wisdom, let him ask of God, who giveth to all liberally and upbraideth not; and it shall be given him. But let him ask in faith, nothing doubting, for he that doubteth is like the surge of the sea driven by the wind and tossed. For let not that man think that he shall receive anything of the Lord.

James 1:5-7. (E.R.V.)

The night is far spent, and the day is at hand: Let us therefore cast off the works of darkness, and let us put on the armor of light.   Rom. 13:12.

The Lord giveth wisdom; out of his mouth cometh knowledge and understanding.   Prov. 2:6.

The entrance of thy words giveth light; it giveth understanding unto the simple.

Ps. 119:130.

Ye shall seek me, and find me, when ye shall search for me with all your hearts.   Jer. 29:13.

He that diligently seeketh good procureth favor; but he that seeketh mischief, it shall come unto him.   Prov. 11:27.

Howbeit in vain do they worship me, teaching for doctrines the commandments of men.

Mark 7:7.

Search the scriptures.   John 5:39.

Search it for the Truth. To be bound to a form of words is slavish idolatry.

Jesus answered and said unto them, Ye do err, not knowing the scriptures, nor the power of God.

Matt. 22:29.

Then opened he their understanding, that they might understand the scriptures.   Luke 24:45.

Verily, verily, I say unto you, The hour is coming, and now is, when the dead shall hear the voice of the Son of God: and they that hear shall live.

John 5:25.

And we know that the Son of God is come, and hath given us an understanding, that we may know him that is true, and we are in him that is true, even in his Son Jesus Christ. This is the true God and eternal life.

1 John 5:20.

I am come a light into the world, that whosoever believeth on me should not abide in the darkness.

John 12:46.

They that seek the Lord understand all things.

Prov. 28:5.

There is no wisdom nor understanding, nor counsel against the Lord.

Prov. 21:30.

A good understanding have all they that do his commandments.

Ps. 111:10.

The wisdom of the prudent is to understand his way.

Prov. 14:8.

Ye have an anointing from the Holy One, and ye know all things.

1 John 2:20. (E.R.V.)

God hath revealed them unto us by his Spirit: for the Spirit searcheth all things, yea, the deep things of God. 1 Cor. 2:10.

For God hath not given us the spirit of fear, but of power, and of love, and of a sound mind.
2 Tim. 1:7.

Thou gavest also thy good spirit to instruct them.
Neh. 9:20.

There is a spirit in man; and the inspiration of the Almighty giveth them understanding.
Job 32:8.

Cease from thine own wisdom. Prov. 23:4.

For the wisdom of this world is foolishness with God. For it is written, He taketh the wise in their own craftiness. And again, The Lord knoweth the thoughts of the wise, that they are vain. Therefore, let no man glory in men. 1 Cor. 3:19-21.

The wise men are ashamed, they are dismayed and taken: lo, they have rejected the word of the Lord; and what wisdom is in them? Jer. 8:9.

The secret of the Lord is with them that fear him;
and he will show them his covenant.

Ps. 25:14.

⌒

In the hidden part thou shalt make me to know
wisdom. Ps. 51:6.

Understanding is a well-spring of life unto him
that hath it. Prov. 16:22.

⌒

Give me understanding, and I shall live.

Ps. 119:144.

To have understanding is to know a way out of
trouble, and to know how to live in peace and
health while we are upon earth. The man that
wandereth out of the way of understanding shall
rest in the congregation of the dead (Prov. 21:16,
E.R.V.).

And none of the wicked shall understand; but the
wise shall understand. Dan. 12:10.

Discretion shall watch over thee; understanding shall keep thee.   Prov. 2:11. (E.R.V.)

Wisdom and understanding are the eyes of Faith—without them Faith is blind.

Knowledge is easy unto him that hath understanding.   Prov. 14:6. (E.R.V.)

Behold the fear of the Lord, that is wisdom; and to depart from evil is understanding.

Job 28:28.

But they regard not the work of the Lord, neither have they considered the operation of his hands. Therefore, my people are gone into captivity because they have no knowledge.

Isa. 5:12-13.

The Fear of Jehovah is the beginning of wisdom; and the knowledge of the Holy (One) is understanding.   Prov. 9:10.

Who is wise and understanding among you? Let him show by his good life his works in meekness of wisdom. But if ye have bitter jealousy and faction in your heart, glory not and lie not against the truth. This wisdom is not a wisdom that cometh down from above but is earthly, sensual, devilish. For where jealousy and faction are, there is confusion and every vile deed.

James 3:13-16. (E.R.V.)

For wisdom is a defense, even as money is a defense; but the excellency of knowledge is, that wisdom preserveth the life of him that hath it.

Eccl. 7:12. (E.R.V.)

For by me thy days shall be multiplied, and the years of thy life shall be increased.

Prov. 9:11.

The tongue of the wise is health.   Prov. 12:18.

They that are after the flesh do mind the things of the flesh.   Rom. 8:5.

To be carnally minded is death; but to be spiritually minded is life and peace.   Rom. 8:6.

All fleshly (sensual) desire has but one tendency, the destruction of the flesh. Unfortunately however, death of the physical body does not destroy such desire. Imagine the hell of the unsatisfied glutton! Blessed are the dead who die in the Lord (Rev. 14:13), who having become "transformed by the renewing of their minds" before what is called death of the body have not these consuming desires to torture them thereafter. Spiritual understanding puts to death fleshly desire, this is "the first death." He that overcometh shall not be hurt of the second death (Rev. 2:11), for the flesh will have lost its importance, and its passing be but an incident in the progression of life.

          ◠

The wise in heart will receive commandments.
Prov. 10:8.

Give instruction to a wise man, and he will be yet wiser; teach a just man and he will increase in learning. For by me (wisdom) thy days shall be multiplied, and the years of thy life shall be increased.   Prov. 9:9, 11.

The law of the wise is a fountain of life, to depart from the snares of death. Good understanding giveth favor.   Prov. 13:14-15.

Through wisdom is a house builded, and by understanding it is established. And by knowledge shall the chambers be filled with all precious and pleasant riches.

Prov. 24:3-4.

Wisdom is a strength to the wise man more than ten rulers that are in a city.

Eccl. 7:19.

A wise man is strong; yea, a man of knowledge increaseth strength.   Prov. 24:5.

☞

If a man (reasoning with his so-called human intelligence) thinketh himself (his mental, mortal self) to be something, when he is nothing he deceiveth himself.   Gal. 6:3.

If one thinks that his strength lies in his nerves and muscles, and truth in the testimony of his senses, he really has no understanding of what is true concerning himself. A sunbeam strikes the reflecting prism and makes it appear to be alive. A ray of divine Light strikes a fleshly body, and the body appears to be intelligent, to act of itself, and to be alive. But the truth is, the prism and the flesh are as one, both matter, sensationless, dead. Mortal man not seeing the individual ray of light, but only the reflection, mistakes the one for the other; not seeing God (the one Power and the one Life), but only His manifestations, he believes that each animated object has an existence all its own. The real life of the prism is in the sunbeam, the real life of the flesh is in the ray of divine Light that issues forth from God carrying Life, Love and all other divine attributes. These rays are his ideas, His children the true selves of each one of us.

To the wise the way of life goeth upward.

Prov. 15:24. (E.R.V.)

For though we walk in the flesh, we do not war according to the flesh, for the weapons of our warfare are not of the flesh, but mighty before God to the casting down of strongholds; casting down reasonings and every high thing that is exalted against the knowledge of God, and bringing every thought into captivity to the obedience of Christ.

2 Cor. 10:3-5. (E.R.V.)

Wherefore think ye evil in your hearts?

Matt. 9.4.

Dislodge an evil thought immediately. To replace it with one of love or gratitude is the true, the ideal way. But evil must not be harbored in a single moment even though you can dislodge it only by fixing the attention upon some material object at hand, carefully noting its size, color and other characteristics. When once the intruder has fled fill the mind with love and gladness. To open the door to one sort of evil may be to let in different forms of it at the same time that settling in unsuspected places may later spring forth into trouble. Then you will ask, "How happened this to come to me?"

He that hath knowledge spareth his words; and a man of understanding is of an excellent spirit.

Prov. 17:27.

Unto you is given to know the mystery of the kingdom of God; but unto them that are without, all these things are done in parables.

Mark 4:11.

But we speak the wisdom of God in a mystery, even the hidden wisdom, which God ordained before the world unto our glory. Which none of the princes of this world knew; for had they known it, they would not have crucified the Lord of glory.

1 Cor. 2:7-8.

Happy is the man that findeth wisdom, and the man that getteth understanding: For the merchandise of it is better than the merchandise of silver, and the gain thereof than fine gold. She is more precious than rubies: and all the things thou canst desire are not to be compared unto her. Length of days is in her right hand; and in her left hand riches and honor. Her ways are ways of pleasantness, and all her paths are peace. She is a tree of life to them that lay hold upon her: and happy is every one that retaineth her. The Lord by wisdom hath rounded the earth; by understanding hath he established the heavens. By his knowledge the depths are broken up, and the clouds drop down the dew. My son, let not them depart from thine eyes: keep sound wisdom and discretion: so shall they be life unto thy soul, and grace to thy neck. Then shalt thou walk in thy way safely, and thy foot shall not stumble. When thou liest down, thou shalt not be afraid: yea, thou shalt lie down, and thy sleep shall be sweet.

Prov. 3:13-24.

Whoso is wise, and will observe these things, even they shall understand the lovingkindness of the Lord. Ps. 107:43.

☞

The earth shall be filled with the knowledge of the glory of the Lord, as the waters cover the sea.

Hab. 2:14.

☞

So shall the knowledge of wisdom be unto thy soul: when thou hast found it, then shall there be a reward, and thy expectation shall not be cut off.

Prov. 24:14.

ASK AND YE SHALL RECEIVE

Thy will be done, as in heaven, so on earth.
                                            Matt. 6:10.

You, not of the flesh, but the real, spiritual, eternal
You, have a distinct place in the divine economy,
and were created for a special purpose. This being
the case, you can readily understand that it is of the
utmost importance that God's will shall be done
concerning you, and that nothing else is of compa-
rable consequence.

Submit yourselves therefore to God.
                                            James 4:7.

Into thy hands I commit my spirit.   Ps. 31:5.

Let every soul be in subjection to the higher powers; for there is no power but of God.
                                    Rom. 13:1. (E.R.V.)

And when ye stand praying, forgive, if ye have aught against any. Mark 11:25.

If I regard iniquity in my heart, the Lord will not hear me. Ps. 66:18.

And all things whatsoever ye shall ask in prayer, believing, ye shall receive.

Matt. 21:22.

If thou canst believe, all things are possible to him that believeth. Mark 9:23.

What things soever ye desire, when ye pray, believe that ye receive them, and ye shall have them.

Mark 11:24.

The eyes of many are closed, and they do not know that a supply for every need is at hand. Through understanding, our eyes are opened, and then we may see to lay hold of the blessings that were all of the time within our reach.

But let him ask in faith, nothing doubting; for he that doubteth is like the surge of the sea driven by the wind and tossed. For let not that man think that he shall receive anything of the Lord; a double minded man, unstable in all his ways.

James 1:6-7. (E.R.V.)

Do not beg of God as though you were doubtful about His answering your prayer, but be certain that your desire will be fulfilled—*if it be His will*. To pray to God while doubting Him is to take His name in vain.

Ask and it shall be given you, seek and ye shall find, knock and it shall be opened unto you.

Matt. 7:7-8.

Be more and more persistent in your efforts to gain understanding—ask, seek, knock.

Verily, verily I say unto you, whatsoever ye shall ask the Father in my name, he will give it you.

John 16:23.

If ye shall ask anything in my name I will do it.

John 14:14.

If you ask in the name of Truth (Christ)—the truth that all you need is awaiting you—you will be shown how to lay hold of it.

Ask, and ye shall receive, that your joy may be full.
John 16:24.

Ye lust and have not; ye kill and are jealous, and cannot obtain: ye fight and war; ye have not because ye ask not. Ye ask and receive not, because ye ask amiss, that ye may spend it in your pleasures.
James 4:2-3. (E.R.V.)

The pleasures of this world—of the flesh—are always followed sooner or later by pain; they never make "the joy full." On the contrary, bitterness never trails after pleasures that come through the workings of spiritual law.

In nothing be anxious; but in everything by prayer and supplications with thanksgiving let your requests be made known unto God.
Phil. 4:6. (E.R.V.)

Pray without ceasing.   1 Thes. 5:17.

Perpetually to long to know the Truth, to wish to be consciously at one with Good—with God and earnestly to wish to manifest Him—is to be ever in a state of uplifting desire—"to pray without ceasing."

Praying always with all prayer and supplication in the Spirit.   Eph. 6:18.

Men ought to always pray, and not to faint.
                                               Luke 18:1.

In all thy ways acknowledge him and he will make plain thy paths.   Prov. 3:6.

When we assert a truth such as "God is ever-present Good," or even when we are denying the seeming power of evil, we are "acknowledging Him;" and we should do so whenever we have a work to do, or an obstruction to remove.

Continue steadfastly in prayer, watching therein with thanksgiving.   Col. 4:2. (E.R.V.)

Watch ye therefore, and pray always, that ye may be accounted worthy to escape all these things that shall come to pass.   Luke 21:36.

☞

And when thou prayest, thou shalt not be as the hypocrites are: for they love to pray standing in the synagogues and in the corners of the streets, that they may be seen of men. Verily I say unto you, They have their reward. But thou, when thou prayest, enter into thy closet, and when thou hast shut thy door, pray to thy Father which is in secret; and thy Father which seeth in secret shall reward thee openly. But when ye pray, use not vain repetitions, as the heathen do: for they think that they shall be heard for their much speaking. Be not ye therefore like unto them: for your Father knoweth what things ye have need of, before ye ask him. After this manner therefore pray ye: Our Father which art in heaven, Hallowed be thy name. Thy kingdom come. Thy will be done on earth, as it is in heaven. Give us this day our daily bread. And forgive us our debts, as we forgive our debtors. And lead us not into temptation, but deliver us from evil: For thine is the Kingdom, and the power, and the glory, for ever. Amen.

Matt. 6:5-13.

⌒

Pray one for another that ye may be healed. The effectual, fervent prayer of a righteous man availeth much. James 5:16.

If any of you lack wisdom, let him ask of God, that giveth to all men liberally, and upbraideth not; and it shall be given him.

James 1:5.

Behold, I am the Lord, the God of all flesh: is there anything too hard for me?

Jer. 32:27.

🙠

Ask ye of the Lord rain in the time of the latter rain; so the Lord shall make bright clouds, and give them showers of rain, to everyone grass in the field.

Zech. 10:1.

The desire of the righteous shall be granted.

Prov. 10:24.

Do not refuse a message of Truth because it comes to you through lips that you have thought of as vile. Never forget that vileness, like any other sin, is but a cloud that hides from view the perfect man. Truth, however, can pierce anything, and it will reach you through everything if you but earnestly desire it.

And whatsoever we ask we receive of him, because we keep his commandments and do those things that are pleasing in his sight.   1 John 3:22.

Call unto me, and I will answer thee, and shew thee great and mighty things, which thou knowest not.
                                             Jer. 33:3.

They that seek the Lord shall not want any good thing.   Ps. 34:10.

The Lord is good unto them that wait for him, to the soul that seeketh him.
                                             Lam. 3:25.

The Lord is nigh unto all them that call upon him, to all that call upon him in truth.
                                             Ps. 145:18.

Take your petition into the quietest place that you know—into the innermost chamber of your being, shut the door of the material world, and when you feel yourself alone with God acknowledge your desire. It may be very trivial. As our understanding grows our desires will change. The boy wishes toys, the man has put away childish things. Presently we shall know the true from the false, the needful from the needless. We must be patient with ourselves and force nothing. Hence, even though your wish is trivial, express it and then be certain that it shall be granted—if it is in accordance with the divine will. Always make this provision; for one must be humble if one wishes to receive the divine blessing, otherwise one's desires may be realized to one's hurt—though not through God, He sends only good, but through one's own vicious will.

☙

But my God shall supply all your need according to his riches in glory by Jesus Christ.

Phil. 4:19.

He shall call upon me, and I will answer him; I will be with him in trouble: I will deliver him and honor him; with long life will I satisfy him, and show him my salvation.

Ps. 91:15-16.

Thou drawest near in the day that I called upon thee; thou saidst, Fear not.

Lam. 3:57.

With God nothing shall be impossible.

Luke 1:37.

⌒

And whatsoever ye shall ask in my name, that will I do, that the Father may be glorified in the Son. If ye shall ask anything in my name, I will do it.

John 14:13-14.

I know that even now whatsoever thou wilt ask of God, God will give it thee.

John 11:22.

If ye abide in me, and my words abide in you, ye shall ask what ye will, and it shall be done unto you.

John 15:7.

This is the confidence that we have in him: that, if we ask anything according to his will, he heareth us. And if we know that he hear us, whatsoever we ask, we know that we have the petitions that we desired of him.

1 John 5:14-15.

Again I say unto you, That if two of you shall agree on earth as touching any thing that they shall ask, it shall be done for them of my Father which is in heaven. For where two or three are gathered together in my name, there am I in the midst of them.

Matt. 18:19-20.

The eyes of all wait upon thee, and thou givest them their meat in due season. Thou openest thine hand, and satisfiest the desire of every living thing.

Ps. 145:15-16.

Thou shalt also decree a thing and it shall be established unto thee. Job 22:28.

Stoutly maintain that all good is yours—every phase of it; and firmly deny that anything can interfere with its manifestation in every detail of your life.

⌒

Thou hast given him his heart's desire, and hast not withholden the request of his lips. He asked life of thee, and thou gavest it to him, even length of days for ever and ever.

Ps. 21:2, 4.

Every good giving and every perfect boon is from above, coming down from the Father of lights, with whom can be no variation, neither shadow that is cast by turning.   James 1:17.

⌒

O thou that hearest prayer, unto thee shall all flesh come.   Ps. 65:2.

HE THAT IS THE GREATEST
AMONG YOU SHALL
BE YOUR SERVANT

Prepare ye the way of the Lord; make his paths straight.   Luke 3:4.

All that the "man of the world" knows of God is what he sees of Him in others. Little by little the divine nature is revealed—in a smile, an unselfish act, appreciation, sympathy, forgiveness, charity. Thus we, if we love our neighbor as ourselves, can "prepare the way of the Lord" into his consciousness by showing him love in all of our actions—for God is Love. We can make "straight" this path of the Lord by revealing to our neighbor the good that is within himself, encouraging and nurturing it until the (seeming) evil that has barred the path is overcome with his own good—with God.

Thou shalt love thy neighbor as thyself.
                                                  Matt. 19:19.

(God) hath made of one blood all nations of men.
Acts 17:26.

Be ye kind one to another, tender-hearted, forgiving each other, even as God also in Christ forgave you.   Eph. 4:32. (E.R.V.)

If each one knew how much to his advantage, his profit, his happiness, now, upon this earth, it would be if he obeyed the commands of God, he would certainly strive with all of his power to obey. When we realize this, it is easy to forgive a brother his perverse actions, and to pity him because of his lack of understanding, helping him with love to understand.

Agree with thine adversary quickly, whiles thou art in the way with him; lest at any time the adversary deliver thee to the judge, and the judge deliver thee to the officer, and thou be cast into prison. Verily I say unto thee, Thou shalt by no means come out thence, till thou hast paid the uttermost farthing.
Matt. 5:25-26.

When any difference arises between another and yourself, if possible agree with him at once, surrendering, if necessary and at all consistent, your claims. It is important that you do not offend him. The value you put upon some material condition may become a stumbling block in his pathway to higher things. Show him instead, that your faith in God tells you that man cannot take away from you anything which God cannot give; and that peace of mind is really the one most desirable possession upon earth. If, on the contrary, you do strive merely for the sake of gaining your own point, you will pay a very dear price for it in the end.

Brethren, even if a man be overtaken in any trespass, ye who are spiritual, restore such a one in a spirit of meekness; looking to thyself, lest thou also be tempted.

Gal. 6:1. (E.R.V.)

Admonish the disorderly, encourage the fainthearted, support the weak, be longsuffering toward all. See that none render unto any one evil for evil; but always follow after that which is good, one toward another, and toward all.

1 Thes. 5:14-15. (E.R.V.)

Be not overcome of evil, but overcome evil with good.   Rom. 12:21.

Look for God in your neighbor, and not for that which is not God. If you see a fault, think of the corresponding virtue and act accordingly. If he is what the world calls stingy, imagine him as the embodiment of generosity, and in turn show to him generosity and gratitude. Remember that you cannot let your mind dwell upon your neighbor's faults without harm to yourself. There is only one way: obey the command, overcome evil with good.

⌒

Be ye therefore merciful, as your Father also is merciful. Luke 6:36.

Judge not, and ye shall not be judged; condemn not, and ye shall not be condemned.
Luke 6:37.

Speak not one against another.
James 4:11. (E.R.V.)

If any man thinketh himself to be religious while he bridleth not his tongue but deceiveth his heart, this man's religion is vain.
James 1:26. (E.R.V.)

Let none of you imagine evil in your hearts against his neighbor. Zech. 8:17.

If it be possible, as much as lieth in you, live peaceably with all men. Rom. 12:18.

Let us not therefore judge one another any more; but judge this rather, that no man put a stumbling block or an occasion to fall in his brother's way.
Rom. 14:13.

But love your enemies, and do them good, and lend, never despairing; and your reward shall be great, and ye shall be sons of the Most High: for he is kind toward the unthankful and evil.
Luke 6:35.

Nor rendering evil for evil, or railing for railing, but contrariwise blessing; knowing that ye are thereunto called, that ye should inherit a blessing.
1 Pet. 3:9.

Doing nothing through faction, or through vainglory, but in lowliness of mind each counting other better than himself, not looking each of you to his own things, but each of you also to the things of others. Phil. 2:3-4. (E.R.V.)

The world goes out of its way to humiliate the vain-glorious person, who, if he were not so blinded by self-conceit, would see that his attitude toward himself shows ignorance and a lack of spiritual understanding. Truly he reasons solely with "the mind of the flesh," or else he would know that of himself he could do nothing (1 Cor. 12:6 and Ps. 115:1). As he does not walk in the light of Truth, he stumbles (Acts 12:23) and the world is glad if he falls. The man who has understanding has also humility and he does all for the glory—not of himself—but of God (1 Cor. 10:31).

Now we that are strong ought to bear the infirmities of the weak, and not to please ourselves. Let each one of us please his neighbor for that which is good, unto edifying.

Rom. 15:1-2. (E.R.V.)

Bear ye one another's burdens, and so fulfil the law of Christ. Gal. 6:2.

Rejoice with them that do rejoice, and weep with them that weep. Rom. 12:15.

When you rejoice with one over his good fortune you are truly manifesting God to him, you are showing the Love that is untainted by jealousy or envy. And why should a believer ever be envious? Does he not know that he is provided with all that he needs for comfort and true happiness? Get into sympathy with another for the purpose of learning how best to implant in his soul the glad tidings which as a Christian you are dispensing. Be careful not to make his grief keener. Be tactful. Tact is common kindness greatly refined.

❧

These are the things that ye shall do: Speak ye every man the truth to his neighbor; execute the judgment of truth and peace in your gates.

Zech. 8:16.

That which is gone out of thy lips thou shalt keep and perform.   Deut. 23:23.

The world is watching you. Give it no cause to say that you do not live according to your profession. Prove your faith by your works. Mean what you say

(Matt. 5:37). Keep your word—your promises (Col. 3:9-10).

In all things I gave you an example, how that so laboring ye ought to help the weak, and to remember the words of the Lord Jesus, how he himself said, It is more blessed to give than to receive.

Acts 20:35.

☞

Withhold not good from them to whom it is due, when it is in the power of thine hand to do it. Say not unto thy neighbor, Go, and come again, and tomorrow I will give; when thou hast it by thee.

Prov. 3:27-28.

Never withhold just praise from him to whom it is due, nor from others concerning him. To do so is quite as dishonest as it is to withhold any of his material belongings. Also any assistance that you can render to him belongs to him in the eyes of God—his Father and yours. It is imperative to obey every impulse to be kind, and you will, if you truly desire to be in the service of the Father. Who knows but that you may have been delegated to answer some one's prayer? Never let a debt go unpaid if it is possible to pay it; to do so is to encumber oneself and possibly add greatly to the burden of others (Prov. 22:7, last clause).

Owe no man anything, but to love one another; for he that loveth another hath fulfilled the law.

Rom. 13:8.

Every man according as he purposeth in his heart, so let him give; not grudgingly, or of necessity, for God loveth a cheerful giver.   2 Cor. 9:7.

For whosoever shall give you a cup of water to drink in my name, because ye belong to Christ, verily, I say unto you, he shall not lose his reward.

Mark 9:42.

Give to him that asketh thee, and from him that would borrow of thee, turn not thou away.

Matt. 5:41.

⌒

And in whatsoever house ye enter, first say, Peace be to this house.   Luke 10:5.

Let this benediction be in your heart whenever you come into the presence of another; it will help greatly to bring him and you into sympathetic accord (Phil. 2:2). Shun every one while you "feel irritable." Not only that, but the moment you feel irritability coming upon you, go into the secret chamber of your being and be perfectly quiet (Mark 4:39) until the assurance takes possession of you, that, in heaven where you truly abide, everything moves in perfect harmony. Divine Truth will banish the untruth of material fret. The man who allows himself to be chronically irritable is never a Christian; he is the most cruel of murderers, killing his victims through the multiplicity of his pin pricks.

Peace be within thy walls, and prosperity within thy palaces. For thy brethren and companions' sakes, I will now say, Peace be within thee. Because of the house of the Lord our God I will seek thy good.

Ps. 122:7-9.

But I say unto you, That ye resist not evil: but whosoever shall smite thee on thy right cheek, turn to him the other also. And if any man will sue thee at the law, and take away thy coat, let him have thy

cloak also. And whosoever shall compel thee to go
a mile, go with him twain.   Matt. 5:39-41.

He proves his Christianity who deals successfully
with "the evil," or even "the disagreeable man." If
his Christianity be the Truth, he "turns the other
cheek," thereby demonstrating the unreality of evil,
that it has no power, is nothing to be afraid of, or
to flee from; and he demonstrates the reality and
power of Love by overcoming the evil with good,
with abundant kindness, greatly above that which
was asked or expected.

Give, and it shall be given unto you; good measure,
pressed down, and shaken together, and running
over, shall men give into your bosom. For with the
same measure that ye mete withal it shall be mea-
sured to you again.   Luke 6:38.

When you see another's need give to him, and do
not stop to consider whether or not you will need
the gift at some future time. God will supply your
own needs when they appear.

Of thine own have we given thee.
                    1 Chron. 29:14.

And if thou bestow upon the hungry that which thy soul desireth, and satisfy the afflicted soul; then shall thy light rise in darkness, and thine obscurity be as noonday.

Isa. 58:10. (E.R.V.)

The message which you have for the world is unique. Your combination of temperament, talent, desire and other characteristics makes it so. There is none other like it. It is your particular offering and you alone can bestow it upon humanity. Many hide their message away in a napkin, afraid to give it out, though mankind needs every one.

When you give to another "that which your soul desireth" you are giving actually of yourself, your message is being delivered. Always give the gift which you would like to own.

☞

The stranger that dwelleth with you shall be unto you as one born among you, and thou shalt love him as thyself. Lev. 19:34.

Treat all alike, lovingly. Henceforth know ye no man after the flesh (2 Cor. 5:16). Let not ties of blood nor other relationship be an excuse for a dictatorial attitude. Man was not given dominion over man. Who is my mother, or my brethren? For whosoever shall do the will of God, the same is my brother and my sister, and mother (Mark 3:33, 35).

Execute true judgment, and show mercy and compassions every man to his brother; and oppress not the widow, nor the fatherless, the stranger, nor the poor; and let none of you imagine evil against his brother in your heart.　　　Zech. 7:9-10.

Charge them that are rich in this present world, that they be not high-minded, nor have their hopes set on the uncertainty of riches, but on God, who giveth us richly all things to enjoy; that they do good, that they be rich in good works, that they be ready to distribute, willing to communicate.

1 Tim. 6:17-18. (E.R.V.)

Woe unto him that buildeth his house by unrighteousness, and his chambers by injustice; that useth his neighbor's service without wages, and giveth him not his hire.

Jer. 22:13. (E.R.V.)

If thine enemy be hungry, give him bread to eat; and if he be thirsty, give him water to drink: for thou shalt heap coals of fire upon his head, and the Lord shall reward thee.

Prov. 25:21-22.

And heal the sick that are therein, and say unto them, The kingdom of God is come nigh unto you.

Luke 10.9.

◦

Be pitiful; be courteous.   1 Pet. 3:8.

There is no such a being as a rude Christian— meaning one who shows a lack of courtesy, of politeness—for

> "Politeness is to do and say
> The kindest thing in the kindest way."

Kindness is the outcome of love. Love never gave birth to rudeness. It may come from lack of thought, but it is the Christian's duty to *think*, to be ever watchful that he conduct himself as though he were all Love—it will come true if he assumes it long enough. When he is rude he is not a Christian—not at that moment—for he is not manifesting Christ, who is revealed only through love. (Prov. 15:23).

To give light to them that sit in darkness and in the shadow of death, to guide our feet into the way of peace.   Luke 1:79.

Ye are the light of the world.   Matt. 5:14.

☞

For I long to see you, that I may impart unto you some spiritual gift, to the end ye may be established; that is, that I with you may be comforted in you, each of us by the other's faith, both yours and mine.   Rom. 1:11-12. (E.R.V.)

Let him know, that he which converteth the sinner from the error of his way, shall save a soul from death, and shall hide a multitude of sins.
                                                James 5:20.

But to do good and to communicate forget not: for with such sacrifices God is well pleased.
                                                Heb. 13:16.

Comfort ye, comfort ye my people, saith your God.
Isa. 40:1.

And he said unto them, Go ye into all the world,
and preach the good tidings to the whole creation.
Mark 16:15. (E.R.V.)

Go, stand and speak in the temple to the people all
the words of this Life.

Acts 5:20.

Put them in mind to be subject to principalities and
powers, to obey magistrates, to be ready to every
good work, to speak evil of no man, to be no
brawlers, but gentle, showing all meekness unto all
men.   Titus 3:1-2.

Be not afraid, but speak, and hold not thy peace.
Acts 18:9.

Let us therefore follow after the things which make
for peace, and things wherewith one may edify
another.   Rom. 14:19.

Blessed are the peacemakers, for they shall be
called the children of God.   Matt. 5:9.

The Lord hath given me the tongue of them that are taught, that I may know how to sustain with words him that is weary.

Isa. 50:4. (E.R.V.)

The Spirit of the Lord God is upon me; because the Lord hath anointed me to preach good tidings unto the meek; he hath sent me to bind up the broken hearted, to proclaim liberty to the captives, and the opening of the eyes of them that are bound; to proclaim the acceptable year of the Lord's favor, and the day of vengeance of our God; to comfort all that mourn; to appoint unto them that mourn in Zion, to give unto them a garland for ashes, the oil of joy for mourning, the garment of praise for the spirit of heaviness.

Isa. 61:1-5.

☞

They helped every one his neighbor: and every one said to his brother, Be of good courage. So the carpenter encouraged the goldsmith, and he that smooteth with the hammer him that smote the anvil, saying, It is ready for the soldering: and he fastened it with nails, that it should not be moved.

Isa. 41:6-7.

It is the Christian's imperative duty to give encouragement whenever and wherever he is able; yet how many of those who call themselves followers of Christ take any pains to say the sympathetic, appreciative word? On the contrary, it often appears that the Christian feels it his duty to say that which is discouraging or disagreeable, deeming everything else flattery and of evil. We little know how near to despair our neighbor may be even though he masks it with smiles. An adverse remark may fell him to the ground, whereas he might rise on wings of hope because of our appreciation. There is always something good one may say (Prov. 16:20)—something to lessen the sting of criticism if that seems to be needful. Remember that just praise is a smile of God, and loving criticism, His guiding hand.

A man hath joy by the answer of his mouth; and a word spoken in due season how good it is! The pure speak pleasant words.

Prov. 15:23, 26. (E.R.V.)

The pure in heart see only God (Matt.5:8)—only Good, hence their conversation is not of evil, of imperfection, destruction, death; but of things that are perfect, that make for peace and happiness and spiritual growth.

☞

Pleasant words are as a honey-comb, sweet to the soul, and health to the bones.　　　Prov. 16:24.

A word fitly spoken is like apples of gold in pictures of silver.　　　Prov. 25:11.

For out of the abundance of the heart the mouth speaketh. A good man out of the good treasure of the heart bringeth forth good things.

Matt. 12:34-35.

Finally, be ye all likeminded, sympathetic, loving as brethren, tenderhearted, humbleminded.

1 Pet. 3:8. (E.R.V.)

You need the message your brother carries, be receptive to it. A critical attitude on your part will give him cause to say, "I do not know why but I am never my best with that person." Be lovingly expectant, and without effort the message will come that will bless both him and you.

Let your light so shine before men; that they may see your good works and glorify your Father who is in heaven.   Matt. 5:16.

If we love one another, God dwelleth in us.
1 John 4:12.

Let us not love in word, neither in tongue; but in deed and in truth.   1 John 3:18.

But whoso hath the world's goods and beholdeth his brother in need, and shutteth up his compassion from him, how doth the love of God abide in him? (1 John 3:17). What doth it profit, my brethren, if a man say he hath faith, but have not works? Can that faith save him? If a brother or sister be naked and in lack of daily food and one of you say unto them, Go in peace, be ye warmed and filled; and yet ye give them not the things needful to the body; what doth it profit? Even so faith, if it have not works, is dead in itself (James 2:14-17).

Thou shalt surely give him, and thine heart shall not be grieved when thou givest unto him: because that for this thing the Lord thy God shall bless thee in all thy works, and in all thou puttest thine hand unto. For the poor shall never cease out of the land: therefore I command thee, saying, Thou shalt open thine hand wide unto thy brother, to thy poor, and to thy needy, in thy land.   Deut. 15:10.

⌒

I am made all things to all men, that I might by all means save some.   1 Cor. 9:22.

Give no occasion of stumbling, either to Jews or to Greeks, or to the church of God. Even as I also please all men in all things, not seeking mine own profit, but the profit of the many, that they may be saved.   1 Cor. 10:32-33.

Pure religion and undefiled before God and the Father is this, to visit the fatherless and widows in their affliction, and to keep oneself unspotted from the world.   James 1:27.

Cast thy bread upon the waters; for thou shalt find it after many days.   Eccl. 11:1.

Who comforteth us in all our tribulation, that we may be able to comfort them which are in any trouble, by the comfort wherewith we ourselves are comforted of God.

2 Cor. 1:4.

And the King shall answer and say unto them, Verily I say unto you, Inasmuch as ye have done it unto one of the least of these my brethren, ye have done it unto me.

Matt. 25:40.

☞

He that hath pity upon the poor lendeth unto the Lord; and that which he hath given will he pay him again.

Prov. 19:17.

Whoso mocketh the poor reproacheth his maker; and he that is glad at calamities shall not be unpunished.

Prov. 17:5.

He that goeth about as a talebearer revealeth secrets; but he that is of a faithful spirit concealeth the matter.

Prov. 11:13.

The malicious talebearer is an anomaly in nature. All other animals which thrive upon corruption because they devour it, are benefactors. But through the scandalmonger, corruption is nourished and increased a thousand fold. The one who has the love of God in heart never discusses the errors and sins of another; on the contrary, he does his best to conceal and to destroy them (Luke 6:31; Ps. 32:1).

☞

How beautiful upon the mountains are the feet of him that bringeth good tidings, that publisheth peace, that bringeth good tidings of good, that publisheth salvation, that saith unto Zion, Thy God reigneth.   Isa. 52:7.

Be sure that you carry happiness and glad tidings about with you. If in a solemn and serious manner you say to a man, "Let me prepare you to die that you may live after death," you will be hardly able to get his attention. But if, with enthusiasm, you tell him that you have good news for him, that it is possible for him to have perfect health, to be prosperous and happy here upon this earth, he will eagerly listen for every word. Man longs for help, he wants it now—for today.

Let your speech be always with grace, seasoned with salt, that ye may know how ye ought to answer every man. Col. 4:6.

Every man shall bear his own burden.

Gal. 6:5.

There are diversities of gifts, but the same Spirit.
1 Cor. 12:4.

But now are they many members, but yet one body. The eye cannot say to the hand I have no need of thee, nor again the head to the feet, I have no need of you.

1 Cor. 12:20-21.

It takes all the light in a sunbeam to fill its own angle; each spoke in a wheel can lift but its share of the weight; each child of God carries a different message. Hence there must be no shirking, nor interference with the duty of another, that the whole may be perfect, divine. In the light of all this how foolish is jealousy!

☞

Let each man prove his own work.   Gal. 6:4.

In our efforts to be kind we must be careful not to perform another's duty for him, thereby to deprive him of needful experience. Neither must we allow ourselves to dictate by over-advice or undue influence. Let none of you suffer as. . . a meddler in other men's matters (1 Peter 4:15). Remember you can shine *upon* your brother, but not *for* him.

Study to be quiet and to do your own business and to work with your own hands.

1 Thes. 4:11.

Because he thinks that he "knows best" many a parent not only dictates the way his child's message is to be delivered, but even the message itself. All of which leads to confusion, discouragement, and finally to failure. Instead the parent should ever encourage the good in his child, patiently removing every obstacle in its way, remembering that each one's message comes from God—is divine; and that his child's true self, like his own, is from eternity—two rays of divine Light of exactly the same value, but pointing in different directions.

He that troubleth his own house shall inherit the wind.   Prov. 11:29.

⌒

The Lord's servant must not strive but be gentle towards all, apt to teach, forbearing, in meekness instructing them that oppose themselves; if peradventure God may give them repentance unto the knowledge of the truth.

2 Tim. 2:24-25. (E.R.V.)

Never be drawn into an argument. Your work will not always be with the well-bred (who do not argue). The world deals summarily with the sins of impoliteness, but you must take another course. Nothing but evil ever comes of controversy, for the spirit back of it is never humble, and truth gains access only through humility.

Put on, therefore, as God's elect, holy and beloved, a heart of compassion, kindness, humility, meekness, long suffering; forbearing one another, and forgiving each other if any man have a complaint against any; even as the Lord forgave you, so also do ye: and above all these things put on love which is the bond of perfectness.

Col. 3:12-13. (E.R.V.)

FORGIVE AND YE SHALL BE FORGIVEN

Take heed to yourselves: if thy brother sin, rebuke him; and if he repent, forgive him. And if he sin against thee seven times in the day, and seven times turn again to thee, saying, I repent; thou shalt forgive him.   Luke 17:3-4. (E.R.V.)

All evil must be forgotten, whether it be in you or your brother. To hold perpetually in remembrance your brother's faults and sins, is to create an imperfect, a distorted pattern from which you will be fashioned.

With all lowliness and meekness, with longsuffering, forbearing one another in love.

Eph. 4:2.

One cannot love one's brother as one should and be unforgiving toward him.

Ye have heard that it was said to them of old time,
Thou shall not kill; and whosoever shall kill shall
be in danger of the judgment: but I say unto you,
that every one who is angry with his brother shall
be in danger of the judgment; and whosoever shall
say to his brother, Raca (an expression of con-
tempt), shall be in danger of the council; and
whosoever shall say, Thou fool, shall be in danger
of the hell of fire. If therefore thou art offering thy
gift at the altar, and there rememberest that thy
brother hath aught against thee, leave there thy gift
before the altar, and go thy way, first be reconciled
to thy brother, and then come and offer thy gift.

Matt. 5:21-24. (E.R.V.)

☙

Release, and ye shall be released.

Luke 6:37. (E.R.V.)

☙

Thoughts of evil weigh us down and make our only
burdens. Man changes so rapidly in body and mind
as to be totally incapable of doing today the wrong
which he did yesterday. He is a different person
and should not be judged by his past.

And when ye stand praying, forgive, if ye have aught against any: that your Father also which is in heaven may forgive you your trespasses.

Mark 11:25.

Then said Jesus: Father, forgive them; for they know not what they do.   Luke 23:34.

(Read Matthew 18:21-35.)

BE OF GOOD CHEER, THY SINS BE FORGIVEN THEE

Accept the truth that God made only that which is perfect and everlasting, and firmly establish the thought that matter is but man's belief—the result of a false point of view. Sin, sickness and death belong wholly to matter, hence they, too, must be but false beliefs. All the things of the material world are as far from the realities of the spirit world as the toys of the nursery are from the necessities of the home.

All unrighteousness is sin (1 John 5:17). The thought of foolishness is sin (Prov. 24:9). Then the lust when it hath conceived, beareth sin, and sin when it is full grown bringeth forth death (James 1:15). Sin is a lie against the truth (James 3:14). To know it as such is to rob it of its seeming power to make it nothing. Good and its opposite evil cannot both be true.

The Lord our God is one Lord.   Deut. 6:4.

Thou shalt have no other Gods before me.

Ex. 20:3.

For I know that in me (that is, in my flesh) dwelleth no good thing.   Rom. 7:18.

Ignorant of the truth man puts flesh upon a throne and worships it far more than a heathen ever worshiped his idol of clay or brass; and in reality this flesh is as inert and unknowing as any idol, whether of clay, brass, wood or gold, while life seems to be *in* the flesh, it is only *seeming*. Life is all there is, and Life is God. Sin comes of a false belief, of unright thoughts, of supposing that this idol of flesh is intelligent, has sensations, passions to gratify, can love, be angry and then appeased. Sin is the offering made to this god; sickness and death, its reward.

Repent ye therefore and turn again that your sins may be blotted out.   Acts 3:19. (E.R.V.)

The only way to repent truly is to turn from a belief in the false to a belief in the truth; from a belief in the power of the flesh, to a belief in the Ever-Present, All-Powerful God of Love, and of Infinite knowledge. This is to "blot out" the "mind of the flesh" and its manifestations, sin and sickness, with the Mind of the Spirit—the consciousness of Life Everlasting. With this change to pure, living thought, this vile body will change from corruption to incorruption, this mortal will put on immortality and finally death will be no more, for there will be nothing to die.

☞

The Kingdom of God is at hand: repent ye and believe in the gospel.   Mark 1:15.

Do not hold the idea that you must grow to be much better—have fewer sins, or perhaps, pass out of the body altogether before you can experience this Heaven that is promised, for the blessed fact is that it takes only intense and earnest desire to make the scales fall from your eyes and then you will see that Heaven is all about you, and has always been there for your enjoyment; but you have not known it because the things of the material world have blinded your eyes (Isa. 59:1).

Forgive, and ye shall be forgiven.　　Luke 6:37.

In order to obtain forgiveness one must unite oneself wholly with Good, and therefore must one put away—which is to forgive—all thoughts of evil and discord in connection with one's neighbor as well as that which is connected with oneself.

Then said Jesus, Father, forgive them; for they know not what they do.　　　Luke 23:34.

They had no spiritual understanding.

Jesus said, Neither do I condemn thee: go thy way; from henceforth sin no more.

John 8:11. (E.R.V.)

⌒

I have blotted out as a thick cloud, thy transgressions, and, as a cloud, thy sins: return unto me; for I have redeemed thee.　　　Isa. 44:22.

Sin has no more reality, substance, nor power than a cloud; but it does seem to obscure the real man. However, Love will make the clouds vanish and the real man will be revealed.

But if the wicked turn from all his sins that he hath committed, and keep all my statutes, and do that which is lawful and right, he shall surely live, he shall not die. None of his transgressions that he hath committed shall be remembered against him: in his righteousness that he hath done he shall live.

Ezek. 18:21-22.

God *never* sent affliction as a punishment for sin; in fact He never punishes. (Those who think that He does lack understanding.) A perfect consciousness of our unity with the source of all Good, the Father of all, frees us from sin and delivers us from the consequences of past sins. The trouble is that few of us hold this consciousness for more than a moment—a flash, as it were—then we turn our attention to the flesh and are again under bondage to sin. We always suffer when we break any divine law; but often the punishment seems out of all proportion to the sin itself.

A child has been commanded to remain at home, but he disobeys and goes into the street to play. Suddenly he sees dashing toward him a team of runaway horses. Terrified he starts for home, but he realizes at once and with horror, that his tiny legs can never carry him there in time. In great agony and with all the intensity of his little being, he screams to his father to come and save him. His father, who is never far away, hears his child's cry, rushes to him, and reaches him just as he is about to be trampled to death; and oh, how lovingly he presses him to his bosom as he carries him to home and safety!

If every earthly father with limited love and limited power would so save his child from paying the penalty for disobedience, how much more our Heavenly Father, who is All-Love and All-Power, would be certain to save His child when he cries understandingly to Him for help (Matt. 18:12-13); when he turns from the flesh to the Spirit, from sin to truth—which is repentance.

⌒

Remember ye not the former things, neither consider the things of old.   Isa. 43:18.

Remorse and worry are twin sins, agents of death, among the very worst—the fatal sins. Where they exist is a lack of understanding, a spiritual blindness and an absence of faith, if Christianity at all, then Christianity at a very low ebb. Mere worldly wisdom will prevent one from lingering over a pit into which one has one fallen, as though enjoying the memory of the unfortunate experience. A true Christian is a builder, and has no time to waste in pits, nor in retrospection—only as it may safeguard others. Do not waste time thinking of your past sins. Go to the seat of your trouble, *change your habit of thought*. Make you a new heart and a new spirit; for why will ye die, O house of Israel? For I have no pleasure in the death of him that dieth, saith the Lord Jehovah; wherefore turn yourselves and live (Ezek. 18:31-32). Make amends (Ezek. 33:14-16), and hasten to ask forgiveness (Ps. 34:18), the wrong is more quickly forgotten.

Forgetting the things which are behind and stretching forward to the things which are before, I press on toward the goal unto the prize of the high calling of God in Christ Jesus.

Phil. 3:13-14. (E.R.V.)

⌒

Blessed are the merciful; for they shall obtain mercy.   Matt. 5:7.

By mercy and truth iniquity is atoned for.

Prov. 16:6.

And I will cleanse them from all their iniquity, whereby they have sinned against me; and I will pardon all their iniquities, whereby they have sinned and whereby they have transgressed against me. Jer. 33:8.

Blessed is he whose transgression is forgiven, whose sin is covered. Ps. 32:1.

Behold, I make all things new. Rev. 21:5.

We have lived so long thinking evil, hearing evil and seeing evil, that we view the world as through a glass that is smoked. But when truth takes possession of us, it is as though we are out in the sunlight for the first time, seeing things as they really are, the blue heaven, the green trees and the flowers. It is truly a new heaven and a new earth. Formerly everything was dull and brown.

And the Spirit of the Lord will come upon thee, and thou . . . shalt be turned into another man.

1 Sam. 10:6.

And have put on the new man, which is renewed in knowledge after the image of Him that created him.   Col. 3:10.

When once we give up faith in matter and trust God for everything, then we will be made anew after the pattern of His loveliness.

☞

Behold, it was for my peace that I had great bitterness; but thou hast loved my soul from the pit of nothingness; for thou hast cast all my sins behind my back.   Isa. 38:17. (E.R.V.)

Come now, and let us reason together, saith the Lord: though your sins be as scarlet, they shall be white as snow; though they be red like crimson, they shall be as wool.   Isa. 1:18.

Thy iniquity is taken away, and thy sin is purged.
                                                        Isa. 6:7.

For thou, Lord, art good, and ready to forgive; and plenteous in mercy unto all them that call upon thee.   Ps. 86:5.

And their sins and iniquities will I remember no more. Heb. 10:17.

I, even I, am he that blotteth out thy transgressions for mine own sake; and will not remember thy sins. Isa. 43:25.

The Lord redeemeth the soul of his servants; and none of them that trust in him shall be held guilty. Ps. 34:22.

They have given up their allegiance to the flesh, they are out from under its power, its laws; they are under another, a higher government, and have its protection.

For I will be merciful to their unrighteousness, and their sins and their iniquities will I remember no more. In that he saith, A new covenant, he hath made the first old. Now that which decayeth and waxeth old is ready to vanish away. Heb. 8:12-13.

For behold, I create new heavens and a new earth, and the former shall not be remembered, nor come into mind. Isa. 65:17.

The latter glory of this house shall be greater than the former, said Jehovah Lord of hosts; and in this place will I give peace, saith Jehovah of hosts.

Haggai 2:9.

Therefore if any man is in Christ he is a new creature; the old things are passed away; behold, they are become new.

2 Cor. 5:17. (E.R.V.)

⌒

Awake thou that sleepest, and arise from the dead, and Christ shall shine upon thee.

Eph. 5:14.

Imagine what this awakening means; to learn that all has been but a dream; all of one's mistakes, sins, illnesses, misfortunes; all the woe of the whole world a hideous nightmare, unreal and to be forgotten! Picture the reality: oneself at rest in a kingdom of Love, wholly under the care of the Creator; perfect Health, Peace and Happiness one's own; the Light of truth (Christ) always shining; always a glorious now. This is the Gospel of Good tidings which Jesus brought to earth, and which He commanded should be preached throughout the world, and this is the message which you and I must deliver to those about us in our own peculiar way—the truth which must be expressed and proved in our daily lives, that the children of men (Rom. 9:8) shall know themselves as the children of God, without blot or blemish.

I WILL HELP THEE

Call upon me in the day of trouble: I will deliver thee, and thou shalt glorify me.

Ps. 50:15.

Thou shalt know that I the Lord am thy Savior and thy Redeemer.

Isa. 60:16.

Before the day was I am he; and there is none that can deliver out of my hand.

Isa. 43:13.

Remember that the state of peace and happiness is the natural state of the children of God. Therefore, to ask for help from trouble into happiness is your privilege. Never forget to give God the glory—to praise Him. He does not need it, but you need to give it and others need to hear it.

Ye shall call upon me, and ye shall go and pray unto me, and I will hearken unto you. And ye shall seek me, and find me, when ye search for me with all your heart, and I will be found of you saith the Lord, and I will turn away your captivity.

Jer. 29:12-14.

Thou hast been my high tower and a refuge in the day of my distress. Unto thee, O my strength, will I sing praises (Ps. 59:16-17, E.R.V.). Take refuge in the Almighty. He will shelter and protect you. He will never disappoint. However, do not wait for trouble to force you to Him—everything else having failed; acquaint yourself with Him now (Job 22:21), learn of Him, gain an understanding of spiritual laws. *Trouble can be avoided.*

☞

Submit yourselves, therefore, to God.

James 4:7.

Desire only that His will be done. He knows—and you do not—what is best. His grace is sufficient for you, no matter what comes.

Let not your heart be troubled, ye believe in God, believe also in me.

John 14:1.

For I the Lord thy God will hold thy right hand, saying unto thee, Fear not, I will help thee.

Isa. 41:13.

☙

With God nothing shall be impossible.

Luke 1:37.

If any trouble seems fixed beyond your control, put it into God's hands. If it comes again into your mind, put it back affirming, *"God will perfect that which concerneth me."* Tremendous power lies back of this truth.

Cast thy burden upon the Lord and he will sustain thee.   Ps. 55:22.

Casting all your anxiety upon him, because he careth for you.   1 Pet. 5:7. (E.R.V.)

When trouble seems before you do not act without first seeking the kingdom of heaven, "the kingdom of heaven is within you" and its atmosphere is Peace, Harmony and Love. Be still, perfectly still, and submit yourself to God. Then cling steadfastly to the truth that there is in this Heaven at hand an answer for every prayer, peace for seeming discord and abundant supply for every need.

Therefore I say unto you, What things soever ye desire, when ye pray, believe that ye receive them, and ye shall have them.   Mark 11:24.

Rest in the Lord, and wait patiently for him.
                                                                    Ps. 37:7.

Ye shall not need to fight in this battle; set yourselves, stand ye still, and see the salvation of Jehovah with you.   2 Chron. 20:17.

The Lord shall fight for you, and ye shall hold your peace.   Ex. 14:14.

Be not afraid nor dismayed by reason of this great multitude; for the battle is not yours, but God's.
                                                    2 Chron. 20:15.

Ye shall not fear them; for the Lord your God, he it is that fighteth for you.   Deut. 3:22. (E.R.V.)

To live through understanding is to swim with the tide. You will have to work, but you will not need "to battle." For the Lord your God is he that goeth with you, to fight for you against your enemies, to save you (Deut. 20:4).

☞

I am with thee and no man shall set on thee to hurt thee.   Acts 18:10.

So that we may boldly say, the Lord is my helper, and I will not fear what man shall do unto me.
                                                          Heb. 13:6.

☞

The salvation of the righteous is of the Lord: he is their strength in the time of trouble.
                                                          Ps. 37:39.

The righteous is delivered out of trouble.
                                                          Prov. 11:8.

Turn about and do an act of kindness if seeming trouble depresses you, for by so doing you make yourself a part of the activity of Good, and before you are aware of it your own affairs will have been untangled. Loving service (not meddling) is a panacea for most woes.

Evil pursueth sinners: but to the righteous good shall be repaid.   Prov. 13:21.

Put not your trust in princes, nor in the son of man, in whom there is no help.

Ps. 146:3.

With him is an arm of flesh, but with us is the Lord our God to help us, and to fight our battles.

2 Chron. 32:8.

⌒

Dread not, neither be afraid of them. The Lord your God who goeth before you, he will fight for you, according to all that he did for you in Egypt before your eyes; and in the wilderness, where thou hast seen how that Jehovah thy God bare thee as a man doth bear his son, in all the way that ye went, until ye came into this place.   Deut. 1:29-31.

Then shalt thou call and the Lord shall answer; thou shalt cry and he shall say: Here I am. If thou take away from the midst of thee the yoke, the putting forth the finger and speaking vanity.

Isa. 58:9.

Nothing can yoke or burden one but one's thoughts—thoughts of hate, of fear, of lust, of greed, of evil in any form. It is better, however, to liken evil thoughts to veils which hide from one's eyes the truth, the beauty of things which grow in the sunshine of Love. These veils are thick and of ugly color. They distort. Many there are who grope about all their lives because they wear such a number; they run into danger, injure themselves and others and finally in seeming darkness they lose their way. The truth is that they were all the time in the light, but they knew it not, for they *would* wear the veils. God acts upon the assumption that every one sees clearly, and who would suspect His ever present help when behind so many thicknesses of evil?

All things work together for good to them that love God.   Rom. 8:28.

The Lord is my shepherd, I shall not want.
                                                            Ps. 23:1.

But my God shall supply all your need according to his riches in glory by Christ Jesus.
                                                            Phil. 4:19.

There is not want to them that fear him.

Ps. 34:9.

I have been young, and now am old; yet have I not seen the righteous forsaken, nor his seed begging bread. Isa. 37:25.

They shall not hunger nor thirst; neither shall the heat nor sun smite them: for he that hath mercy on them shall lead them, even by the springs of water shall he guide them.

Isa. 49:10.

When the poor and needy seek water, and there is none, and their tongue faileth for thirst, I the Lord will hear them, I the God of Israel will not forsake them. I will open rivers in high places, and fountains in the midst of the valleys: I will make the wilderness a pool of water, and the dry land springs of water. Isa. 41:17-18.

There shall no mischief happen to the righteous.

Prov. 12:21. (E.R.V.)

There shall no evil befall thee, neither shall any plague come nigh thy dwelling. Ps. 91:10.

Fear not, for I am with thee. Isa. 43:5.

He that is perfect in knowledge, is with thee.
Job 36:4.

Thou shalt increase my greatness, and comfort me
on every side. Ps. 71:21.

Behold, now is the accepted time; behold, now is
the day of salvation. 2 Cor. 6:2.

Never speak of an opportunity as being lost. There
is no such thing. All possibility awaits you NOW.
The law of Good, like the law of gravity, operates
constantly for every one, and nothing one can do
can change its activity, which is perfect; but we can
interfere with its activity in our behalf with such
obstacles as self-righteousness, false pride, hatred
and other evils.

The Lord raiseth them that are bowed down.
Ps. 146:8.

The angel of the Lord encampeth around about
them that fear him and delivereth them.
Ps. 34:7.

For I am with thee, saith the Lord, to save thee.

Jer. 30:11.

Blessed is the man that trusteth in him.

Ps. 34:8.

∽

God giveth to a man that is good in his sight wisdom, and knowledge, and joy.

Eccl. 2:26.

Who healeth all thy diseases.   Ps. 103:3.

My grace is sufficient for thee, for my strength is made perfect in weakness.

2 Cor. 12:9.

For when I am weak, then am I strong (2 Cor. 12:10). Becoming humble through helplessness, I give myself wholly up to God; then nothing hinders His power from being made perfect in me—then am I strong.

The Lord stood with me, and strengthened me.

2 Tim. 4:17.

As one whom his mother comforteth, so will I comfort you.   Isa. 66:13.

No good thing will he withhold from them that walk uprightly.   Ps. 84:11.

Every plant which my heavenly Father hath not planted shall be rooted up.

Matt. 15:13.

Hence all things that mature into discouragement, sin, sickness, or death shall be rooted up, for these are not of the garden of God.

God is able to make all grace abound toward you; that ye, always having all sufficiency in all things may abound to every good work.   2 Cor. 9:8.

⌒

Whoso hearkeneth unto me shall dwell securely, and shall be quiet without fear of evil.

Prov. 1:33. (E.R.V.)

Preserve my life from fear of the enemy (Ps. 64:1). Fear prevents us from taking hold of Good—we must meet it and deny it. And who is he that will harm you, if ye be followers of that which is good? (1 Pet. 3:13). If God be for us who can be against us? (Rom. 8:31). The Lord is my light and my salvation; whom shall I fear? The Lord is the strength of my life; of whom shall I be afraid? (Ps. 27:1).

Give us help from trouble, for vain is the help of man.   Ps. 60:11.

Are not two sparrows sold for a farthing? And one of them shall not fall on the ground without your Father: but the very hairs of your head are all numbered. Fear ye not, therefore, ye are of more value than many sparrows (Matt. 10:29-31). It is very hard to imagine the nearness and complete-ness of our Father's care and protection. He is our very breath—Life itself.

The Lord is good, a stronghold in the day of trouble; and he knoweth them that trust in him.
                                                            Nah. 1:7.

Oh, that my people would hearken unto me, that Israel would walk in my ways. I should soon subdue their enemies, and turn my hand against their adversaries.   Ps. 81:13-14.

Behold, the Lord's hand is not shortened that it cannot save; neither his ear heavy that he cannot hear; but your iniquities have separated between you and your God, and your sins have hid his face from you, that he will not hear. Isa. 59:1.

When the enemy shall come in like a flood, the Spirit of the Lord shall lift up a standard against him. Isa. 59:19.

He shall call upon me and I will answer him. I will be with him in trouble: I will deliver him and honor him. Ps. 91:15.

God was with him, and delivered him out of all his afflictions. Acts 7:9-10.

Thus, saith the Lord, even the captives of the mighty shall be taken away, and the prey of the terrible shall be delivered; for I will contend with him that contendeth with thee, and I will save thy children. Isa. 49:25.

Behold, all they that are incensed against thee shall be put to shame and confounded; they that strive with thee shall be as nothing, and shall perish.

Thou shalt seek them, and shalt not find them, even them that contend with thee: they that war against thee shall be as nothing, and as a thing of nought.   Isa. 41:11-12.

Thou shalt be hid from the scourge of the tongue.
                                          Job 5:21.

No weapon that is formed against thee shall prosper, and every tongue that shall rise against thee in judgment thou shalt condemn. This is the heritage of the servants of the Lord, and their righteousness is of me, saith the Lord.   Isa. 54:17.

☞

At destruction and dearth thou shalt laugh; neither shalt thou be afraid of the beasts of the earth. For thou shalt be in league with the stones of the field; and the beasts of the field shall be at peace with thee. And thou shalt know that thy tent is in peace.
                              Job. 5:22-24. (E.R.V.)

To him, who follows after Good, who keeps the commandments and who possesses understanding, it appears that everything extends the offer of help, whether animate or inanimate, friend or foe. He maketh even his enemies to be at peace with him (Prov. 16:7).

For thou hast been a strength to the poor, a strength to the needy in his distress, a refuge from the storm, a shadow from the heat, when the blast of the terrible ones is as a storm against the wall.

Isa. 25:4.

For he will deliver the needy when he crieth; and the poor, and him that hath no helper. He will have pity on the weak and needy, and the souls of the needy he will save. He will redeem their soul from oppression and violence, and precious will their blood be in his sight; and they shall live.

Ps. 72:12-15.

All my bones shall say, Lord, who is like unto thee, which deliverest the poor from him that is too strong for him, yea, the poor and the needy from him that spoileth him?

Ps. 35:10.

I sought the Lord, and he answered me, and delivered me from all my fears. They looked unto him, and were lightened: and their faces shall never be confounded. This poor man cried, and the Lord heard him, and saved him out of all his troubles.

Ps. 34:4-6.

Mine eyes are ever toward the Lord; for he shall pluck my feet out of the net.

Ps. 25:15.

The Lord upholdeth all that fall, and raiseth up all those that be bowed down. The eyes of all wait upon thee; and thou givest them their meat in due season. Thou openest thine hand, and satisfiest the desire of every living thing.

Ps. 145:14, 16.

⌒

I will go before thee and make the rugged places plain; I will break in pieces the doors of brass, and cut in sunder the bars of iron, and I will give thee the treasures of darkness, and hidden riches of secret places. Isa. 45:2-3.

Hast thou not known? hast thou not heard? that the everlasting God, the Lord, the Creator of the ends of the earth, fainteth not, neither is weary; there is no searching of his understanding.

Isa. 40:28.

Thou was wearied with the length of thy way; yet saidst thou not, there is no hope: thou didst find a quickening of thy strength, therefore thou wast not faint.

Isa. 57:10.

☜

Except the Lord build the house, they labor in vain that build it: Except the Lord keep the city, the watchman waketh but in vain. It is vain for you that ye rise up early, and so late take rest, And eat the bread of toil: For so he giveth unto his beloved in sleep.

Ps. 127:1-2. (E.R.V.)

In all thy ways acknowledge him, and he will make plain thy paths.   Prov. 3:6.

When thou passest through the waters, I will be with thee; and through the rivers, they shall not overflow thee; when thou walkest through the fire,

thou shalt not be burned; neither shall the flame
kindle upon thee.   Isa. 43:2.

He maketh the storm a calm, so that the waves
thereof are still.   Ps. 107:29.

For I am persuaded, that neither death, nor life,
nor angels, nor principalities, nor powers, nor
things present, nor things to come, nor height, nor
depth, nor any other creature, shall be able to
separate us from the love of God, which is in
Christ Jesus, our Lord.

Rom. 8:38-39.

✑

And I will pray the Father, and he shall give you
another Comforter, that he may abide with you
forever; even the Spirit of truth; whom the world
cannot receive, because it seeth him not, neither
knoweth him, but ye know him; for he dwelleth
with you, and shall be in you.

John 14:16-17.

Thus saith God the Lord, he that created the
heavens, and stretched them out; he that spread

forth the earth, and that which cometh out of it; he
that giveth breath unto the people upon it, and
spirit to them that walk therein. I, the Lord, have
called thee in righteousness, and will hold thine
hand, and will keep thee, and give thee for a covenant of the people.   Isa. 42:5-6.

Cursed be the man that trusteth in man, and
maketh flesh his arm and whose heart departeth
from the Lord; for he shall be like the heath in the
desert, and shall not see when good cometh; but
shall inhabit the parched places in the wilderness,
a salt land and not inhabited.   Jer. 17:5.

I, even I, am he that comforteth you: who art thou,
that thou shouldest be afraid of a man that shall
die, and of the son of man which shall be made as
grass; and forgettest the Lord thy Maker, that hath
stretched forth the heavens, and laid the founda-
tions of the earth; and hast feared continually every
day because of the fury of the oppressor, as if he
were ready to destroy? and where is the fury of the
oppressor?   Isa. 51:12-14.

The Lord said unto my Lord, Sit thou at my right
hand, till I make thine enemies thy footstool.
                                    Ps. 110:1.

When he giveth quietness who then can make trouble?   Job 34:29.

When thou art in tribulation and all these things are come upon thee, if in the latter days thou return to the Lord thy God, and hearken unto his voice: for the Lord thy God is a merciful God; he will not fail thee, neither destroy thee.

Deut. 4:30.

Only goodness and loving kindness shall follow me all the days of my life; and I shall dwell in the house of Jehovah forever.

Ps. 23:6. (E.R.V.)

Read over and over Psalms 1, 34, 91, 145, and 146; they are filled with assurances of help.

BEHOLD, I WILL HEAL THEE

Be ye transformed by the renewing of your mind.
Rom. 12:2.

Let the wicked forsake his way and the unrighteous
man his thoughts (Isa. 55:7). These are the first
commandments that you must obey if you would be
in conscious health. Devotion to matter must cease
(Ex. 20:3), and our habit of thought concerning
the physical body—that it has life, power, and is
substance—must be changed. We must separate it
in our thoughts from that which God has made
(Rom. 9:8), for flesh decays and dies, while all of
God's creation (and He is the only Creator) is
perfect and eternal (Eccl. 3:14). A philosopher, a
bishop of England, declared over two hundred
years ago that "Matter cannot be conceived to exist,
the only possible substance being Mind." And the
scientist today is not far from this conclusion when
he reduces the atom, of which matter is thought to

be composed, to a form of energy, unseen and as yet unknown.

If our higher consciousness cannot now conceive of flesh as a reality and of God, it must be that we have been misled in the past by our lower consciousness, the "mind of the flesh"; and when we consider that this lower mind bases its opinions and decisions solely upon the testimony of the senses—which we know to be unreliable—we wonder that we could have been deceived. It is from the "mind of the flesh" that the carnal law, the law of sin, comes forth; which, presuming sensation in our really insensible bodies; decrees that certain things shall give pleasure; other things shall give pain; some things shall cause sickness, other things shall cure it. This "mind of the flesh," identified as it is with the darkness of untruth, is at enmity against the Good (Rom. 8:6-8), and is the seat of all "evil imaginings." Rejoicing in them, it "perverts the right ways of the Lord" and "seeks out many inventions." Being a deceiver, like the ventriloquist who projects his voice into the wooden manikin and makes it appear to talk, this "mind of the flesh" projects a thought of sickness, of pain, or of pleasure into some part of the physical body and makes that part appear to be sick, to have pain or pleasure. Thus does it bind us in every way to the false, to that which will surely destroy us. Hence in order to be in perfect health, to have peace and happiness, we must be lifted out of this "mind of the flesh" into the Mind of the Spirit which is life and truth; and we do so by giving up our belief in matter and by refusing to be governed by the physical senses. This will release us from our bondage to fear, and free us from the law of sin which decrees sickness and death.

Ye shall know the truth and the truth shall make you free.

John 8:32.

A realization of the truth will banish every ill. It is the light which reduces darkness to nothingness. Apply the truth to evil, and the evil disappears.

If you are not in conscious health, clear away your mental darkness by the knowledge that you are not under any so-called law or penalty of the flesh. You are under the law of God which decrees health and happiness.

I am the Lord that healeth thee.

Ex. 15:26.

Ye shall seek me, and find me, when ye search for me with all your heart. Jer. 29:13.

If thou return to the Almighty, thou shalt be built up. Job 22:23.

Hold fast to this thought: *All healing power comes from God*, and is ever present with you awaiting your recognition.

⌒

In whose hand is the soul of every living thing and the breath of all mankind.

Job 12:10.

The Lord will perfect that which concerneth me.

Ps. 138:8.

There is a perpetual working of the Perfect Law of God. Whether one receives a blessing from it or not depends largely upon one's appreciation and recognition.

No word from God shall be void of power.

Luke 1:37. (E.R.V.)

Remember that power is exerted by merely *stating* a truth. All truth is the word of God. Assert it constantly, even though your so-called human mind screams "falsehood" (Rom. 8:6, E.R.V.). It is to acknowledge Him—to have your mind stayed on Him—to be directly benefited by the activity of Good.

I will cry unto God Most High, unto God that performeth all things for me. He shall send from heaven and save me. . . God shall send forth his mercy and his truth.

Ps. 57:2-3.

For I, the Lord, change not.   Mal. 3:6.

The same yesterday, today and forever. The power of God, whether manifested in healing, replacement, growth, or in the various functions, is constant, regular, gentle, never failing. Give yourself up to it body and mind, trust it wholly if in it you would breath, move, and sustain your being.

Behold, I am the Lord, the God of all flesh: is there anything too hard for me?

Jer. 32:27.

Has the Lord, who made all things, made something for which He cannot care? He perfectly governs all He has created.

I will restore health unto thee, and I will heal thee of thy wounds, saith the Lord (Jer. 30:17). Who healeth all thy diseases. Who satisfieth thy mouth with good things; so that thy youth is renewed like the eagle (Ps. 103:3, 5).

☙

But that ye may know that the Son of man hath power on earth to forgive sins, (then saith he to the sick of the palsy,) Arise, and take up thy bed, and go unto thy house, and he arose and departed to his house.   Matt. 9:6-7.

With long life will I satisfy him, and show him my salvation.   Ps. 91:16.

Even to old age I am he, and even to hoar hairs will I carry you; I have made and I will bear; yea, I will carry, and will deliver.   Isa. 46:4. (E.R.V.)

Unto God the Lord belong the issues (escape) from death.   Ps. 68:20.

He shall gently lead those that are with young.

Isa. 40:11.

O Lord, thou preservest man and beast.

Ps. 36:6.

The Lord will strengthen him upon his bed of languishing. Ps. 41:3.

☞

I will ransom them from the power of the grave: I will redeem them from death. Hos. 13:14.

Deliver them all who through fear of death were all their lifetime subject to bondage.

Heb. 2:15.

For by me thy days shall be multiplied, and the years of thy life shall be increased.

Prov. 9:11.

Bloody and deceitful men shall not live out half their days (Ps. 55:23). Fools, because of their transgression, and because of their iniquities, are afflicted (Ps. 107:17).

Unto you that fear my name shall the sun of righteousness arise with healing in his wings.

Mal. 4:2.

It shall not be well with the wicked, neither shall he prolong his days, which are as a shadow; because he feareth not before God.

Eccl. 8:13.

For my people have committed two evils: they have forsaken me, the fountain of living waters, and hewed them out cisterns, broken cisterns, that can hold no water. Jer. 2:13.

Behold, I will bring it health and cure, and I will cure them; and will reveal unto them abundance of peace and truth. Jer. 33:6.

Then they cry unto the Lord in their trouble, and he saveth them out of their distresses. He sent his word and healed them, and delivered them from their destructions.

Ps. 107:19-20.

Behold, I make all things new.

Rev. 21:5.

Physiologists tell us that every cell in the human body is replaced by a new one every few months, that we are actually, wholly remade. We are further informed by scientists of another sort that whether or not the new cell is perfect, rests entirely with us—with the "mind of the flesh"—its character is determined by that which we hold in our thoughts. Thus if health and perfection are in our consciousness, health and perfection will be manifested. If, however, we picture disease and imperfection—then these things are likely to appear.

⌒

I will put my Spirit in you, and ye shall live.
Ezek. 37:14. (E.R.V.)

If you believe that God has sent affliction for your good your belief has bound you to a rack of torture, and you must endure it—until the truth frees you, the truth that God never resorts to evil to bring about His purpose; but that His activity works only good, always and to every one, never changing, never detouring, never making exceptions, but is an ever-flowing river of Life; and he who understands this truth is like a tree planted by its side "whose leaf also shall not wither" (Ps. 1:3), whose "soul shall be like a watered garden, and he shall not sorrow any more at all" (Jer. 31:12).

For the law of the Spirit of life in Christ Jesus hath made me free from the law of sin and death.

Rom. 8:2.

But if the Spirit of Him that raised up Jesus from the dead dwelleth in you, he that raised up Christ Jesus from the dead shall give life also to your mortal bodies because of his Spirit that dwelleth in you (Rom. 8:11). For if ye live after the flesh, after its decisions and abide by its laws, ye *must* die; but if by the strength of the Spirit your consciousness is lifted up from the flesh to God, from the false to the true, ye shall live. The higher law of truth makes null and void any so-called human law.

It is the Spirit that giveth life; the flesh profiteth nothing: the words that I have spoken unto you are spirit, and are life. John 6:63.

The Spirit also helpeth our infirmities.

Rom. 8:26.

Exercise thyself rather unto Godliness, for bodily exercise profiteth little: but godliness is profitable unto all things, having promise of the life that now is, and of that which is to come.   1 Tim. 4:7-8.

⌒

Be subject therefore unto God.   James 4:7.

Into his hands deliver thyself without reservation. Believe His promises. Know no other law than His, write it upon the tablet of thy heart (Prov. 3:3).

Be still, and know that I am God.   Ps. 46:10.

Shut out the noise and confusion of the material world, and let the consciousness that the Spirit of God possesses you, become clear.

Thou wilt keep him in perfect peace whose mind is stayed on thee.   Isa. 26:3.

Think as little as possible of the physical body, keep the mind stayed upon your perfect spiritual being made in the image and likeness of God, the ray of divine Light that proceeds from His very Self's substance, the living intelligent You that is quite apart from the flesh.

If thou wilt enter into Life, keep the commandments.   Matt. 19:17.

My son, attend to my words; incline thine ear unto
my sayings. Let them not depart from thine eyes;
keep them in the midst of thine heart. For they are
life unto those that find them, and health to all
their flesh. Keep thy heart with all diligence; for
out of it are the issues of life. Put away from thee
a wayward mouth, and perverse lips put far from
thee. Let thine eyes look right on, and let thine
eyelids look straight before thee. Weigh carefully
the path of thy feet, and let all thy ways be ordered
aright. Turn not to the right hand nor to the left:
remove thy foot from evil.
                          Prov. 4:20-27. (E.R.V.)

Set your heart unto all the words which I testify
unto you this day, which ye shall command your
children to observe to do, all the words of this law.
For it is no vain thing for you; because it is your
life and through this thing ye shall prolong your
days.   Deut. 32:46-47. (E.R.V.)

I call heaven and earth to witness against you this
day, that I have set before thee life and death, the

blessing and the curse; therefore choose life, that thou mayest live, thou and thy seed. To love the Lord thy God, to obey his voice, and to cleave unto him, for he is thy life, and the length of thy days, that thou mayest dwell in the land which the Lord swear unto thy fathers, to Abraham, to Isaac, and to Jacob, to give them.

Deut. 30:19-20. (E.R.V.)

Verily, verily I say unto you, He that heareth my word, and believeth him that sent me, hath eternal life and cometh not into judgment, but hath passed out of death into life.　　　John 5:24. (E.R.V.)

Believe on the Lord Jesus Christ and thou shalt be saved, and thy house.　　　Acts 16:31.

Therefore I say unto you, What things soever ye desire, when ye pray, believe that ye receive them, and ye shall have them.　　　Mark 11:24.

All things are possible to him that believeth.

Mark 9:23.

According to your faith be it done unto you.

Matt. 9:29. (E.R.V.)

And his name, through faith in his name, hath made this man strong, whom ye see and know: yea, the faith which is by him hath given him this perfect soundness in the presence of you all.

Acts 3:16.

And Jesus said unto him, Go thy way; thy faith hath made thee whole. Mark 10:52.

And the prayer of faith shall save the sick, and the Lord shall raise him up; and if he have committed sins, they shall be forgiven him.

James 5:15.

Pray one for another that ye may be healed. The supplication of a righteous man availeth much in its working. James 5:16. (E.R.V.)

I have heard thy prayer, I have seen thy tears: behold, I will heal thee (2 Kings 20:5). I have seen his ways, and will heal him; I will lead him also, and restore comforts unto him and to his mourners (Isa. 57:18).

⌒

Rejoice in the Lord always. Phil. 4:4.

The joy of the Lord is your strength.

Neh. 8:10.

Delight thyself also in the Lord; and he shall give thee the desires of thine heart.　　　Ps. 37:4.

My heart is glad and my glory rejoiceth, my flesh also shall rest in hope.　　　Ps. 16:9.

Be ye thankful.　　　Col 3:15.

Make a daily inventory of your blessings.
Thanksgiving is spiritual activity—the law of Good in operation.

The mind of the flesh is death, but the mind of the Spirit is life and peace.　　　Rom. 8:6. (E.R.V.)

Let this mind be in you which was also in Christ Jesus.　　　Phil. 2:5.

Cease from anger, and forsake wrath: fret not thyself, it tendeth only to evil-doing.

Ps. 37:8. (E.R.V.)

In nothing be anxious.　　　Phil. 4:6. (E.R.V.)

Anxiety, fret, anger and all other such evidences of lack of faith are quick destroyers of the body. They are ideas of "the mind of the flesh," and they do the work of devils.

Resist the devil (evil) and he will flee from you.
James 4:7.

Do not claim a disease either in thought or word. Never say, "My headache, my sore throat," thus entering into partnership with evil. On the other hand resist the first sign of physical disorder, refuse to admit its power or reality, remember man can receive nothing except it have been given him from heaven (John 3:17); but you can *think* the reverse, and your suffering will be in accordance with your thought.

As he thinketh in his heart, so is he.
Prov. 23:7.

After having given it needful care forget your body as far as possible. Think of it only as a symbol, not as *You*. Remember that oft-repeated illustration—the sum upon the blackboard, two times two equals four. The figures of themselves are nothing, but they express an everlasting truth. Rub the figures out yet the truth is unchanged, for two times two equals four whether it is expressed or not. Neither think of your Spiritual Self as having the form of your fleshly self; for to do so is unconsciously to fix a limit—arms reach only so far, eyes see but in one direction, ears hear only so much. Think of yourself in limitless terms of Spirit; as expressing Love, Life, Power, Health, Beauty, All-Possibility, Harmony and other Godly attributes—they are all yours, as much as you are capable of reflecting.

There is no power but of God.   Rom. 13:1.

☞

To admit that disease has you in its grasp is to admit that you believe in a power opposed to God—an acknowledgment that you have broken the first commandment.

God created man in his own image.

Gen. 1:27.

To declare that you are well is to tell the exact truth. You are not flesh, but rather the ray of divine Light that, shining upon flesh, makes it appear alive. This "You" is spiritual, and cannot be sick.

⌒

Finally brethren, whatsoever things are true, whatsoever things are honest, whatsoever things are just, whatsoever things are pure, whatsoever things are lovely, whatsoever things are of good report; if there be any virtue, if there be any praise, think on these things.

Phil. 4:8.

Think upon the things that make a perfect pattern—from which to be renewed (Ps. 101:3, and 2 Tim. 1:13). The thought of foolishness is sin (Prov. 24:9).

Wherefore think ye evil in your hearts? (Matt. 9:4). For as a man thinketh in his heart so he is (Prov. 23:7). For to be carnally minded is death, but to be spiritually minded is life and peace (Rom. 8:6).

God is the strength of my heart.   Ps. 73:26.

A merry heart maketh a cheerful countenance; but by sorrow of the heart the spirit is broken.

Prov. 15:13.

Pleasant words are as a honeycomb, sweet to the soul and health to the bones.　　　Prov. 16:24.

The light of the eyes rejoiceth the heart, and good tidings make the bones fat.

Prov. 15:30. (E.R.V.)

A cheerful heart causeth good healing. But a broken spirit drieth up the bones.

Prov. 17:22. (E.R.V.)

The tongue of the wise is health.

Prov. 12:18.

Cast thy burden upon the Lord, and he shall sustain thee; he shall never suffer the righteous to be moved.　　　Ps. 55:22.

Know that in time of trouble, "it is in the Lord's hands," your relief will be great, help will come. You cannot be in health and bear burdens of any kind.

To declare that a thing is perfect is to recognize the real, though the unseen truth, concerning it; and to declare the truth over and over again is to make it finally manifest as reality.

⌐

They did take their food with gladness and single-ness of heart.   Acts 2:46.

If you cling to the belief that your life is wholly dependent upon material food you are at the mercy of a vicious material law grown out of a belief in the flesh which decrees that certain foods shall agree with you and others shall be injurious. On the contrary you will never suffer from what you eat, if the supreme law of Good is firmly fixed in your consciousness, and if you realize the truth of your being that your life is forever with God, your creator (Job 33:4), preserver (Neh. 9:6), and strength (Isa. 26:4, Hab. 3:19). Man can receive nothing except it be given him from heaven (John 3:27). Therefore eat what is set before you (1 Cor. 10:27, Luke 12:22-24, 29-31), and think nothing of its supposed importance and action, having only "singleness" of purpose, to glorify God (1 Cor. 10:31).

For freedom did Christ set us free: stand fast therefore, and be not entangled again in a yoke of bondage.   Gal. 5:1. (E.R.V.)

Man doth not live by bread only, but by every word that proceedeth out of the mouth of the Lord doth man live.   Deut. 8:3.

All the days of the afflicted are evil; but he that is of a cheerful heart hath a continual feast.

Prov. 15:15.

Seek good and not evil, that ye may live.

Amos 5:14.

Therefore seek for manifestations of goodness, health, beauty and perfection. Cast out all evil thoughts—all that are *not good*. Understand that you grow to be like the image which your thoughts put forth. Do not idly talk of disease, you have no right to place imperfection before the eyes of another, it is to open the doors of his house to those who will rob him. Hold the pattern of healthful words which thou hast heard from me in faith and love which is in Christ Jesus (2 Tim. 1:13). See, saith he, that thou make all things according to the pattern that was shewed thee in the mount (Heb. 8:5), after the vision of perfect beauty which appears only to our highest consciousness.

☙

Glorify God in your body.   1 Cor. 6:20.

Let love and joy radiate from it. Make it beautiful; it is the sanctuary of the Holy Spirit, and must not be used for pleasures wholly fleshly, "perverting the right ways of the Lord" (Acts 13:10). For if ye live after the flesh, ye must die, but if by the Spirit, ye put to death the doings of the body, ye shall live (Rom. 8:13, E.R.V.).

In the way of righteousness is life, and in the pathway thereof there is no death.

Prov. 12:28.

Ye shall serve the Lord your God, and he shall bless thy bread and thy water; and I will take sickness away from the midst of thee. There shall none cast her young, nor be barren in thy land; the number of thy days I will fulfill.

Ex. 23:25-26.

But they that wait upon the Lord shall renew their strength; they shall mount up with wings as eagles; they shall run and not be weary; and they shall walk and not faint.   Isa. 40:31.

Fatigue is the result of a lack of understanding, an ignorance of the truth, a punishment for not observing the law of the Spirit. If before you begin your labors you would "seek the Kingdom of God" you would find your way made plain, your work made easier and much of it done for you.

There shall no mischief happen to the righteous.
                                  Prov. 12:21. (E.R.V.)

As thy days so shall thy strength be.
                                  Deut. 33:25.

The Lord openeth the eyes of the blind.
                                  Ps. 146:8.

The hearing ear, and the seeing eye, the Lord hath made even both of them.   Prov. 20:12.

The eyes of them that see shall not be dim, and the ears of them that hear shall hearken.   Isa. 32:3.

The blind receive their sight, and the lame walk, the lepers are cleansed, and the deaf hear, the dead are raised up, and the poor have the gospel preached to them.   Matt. 11:5.

Thou art loosed from thine infirmity.

Luke 13:12.

I have broken the bands of your yoke, and made you go upright.   Lev. 26:13.

Wherefore make straight the hands that hang down, and the palsied knees; and make straight paths for your feet, that which is lame be not put out of joint, but rather be healed.

Heb. 12:12-13. (E.R.V.)

He shall be like a tree planted by the rivers of water, that bringeth forth his fruit in his season; his leaf also shall not wither.   Ps. 1:3.

There shall be no more thence an infant of days, nor an old man that hath not filled his days; for the child shall die a hundred years old, but the sinner being a hundred years old shall be accursed.

Isa. 65:20.

As man gains spiritual understanding, there shall be no more death in childhood, none prematurely old; but youth with all its perfectness, beauty and charm shall last through all the years; but he who lacks understanding shall continue to grow withered and unlovely in appearance as his years increase.

And his flesh came again like unto the flesh of a little child, and he was clean.   2 Kings 5:14.

Let not sin therefore reign in your mortal body, that ye should obey it in the lusts thereof.

Rom. 6:12.

He (Christ) is the Savior of the body.

Eph. 5:23.

Who shall change our vile body, that it may be fashioned like unto his glorious body, according to the working whereby he is able even to subdue all things unto himself.

Phil. 3:21.

Then shall thy light break forth as the morning, and thy healing shall spring forth speedily; and thy righteousness shall go before thee; the glory of the Lord shall be thy rearward (rearguard).

Isa. 58:8.

His flesh shall be fresher than a child's: he shall return to the days of his youth.

Job 33:25.

Thou shalt come to thy grave in a full age, like as a shock of corn cometh in its season.

Job 5:26.

FOR THINE IS THE POWER

There is no power but of God; the powers that be are ordained of God.   Rom. 13:1.

Persistently affirm that there is no power but of God—but that which is manifested in Good. It will be a usable truth when once you get it fixed in your consciousness, an ever present Help, a Comforter, a Support, a Protection. No evil can come near you, for evil has no power, and is helpless before Good. To believe that it has power and to fear it, is to deny your God, to move away from His protection, to give yourself into the hands of the enemy, to be at the mercy of fate. The power which evil appears to have, comes from the beliefs of "the mind of the flesh"—is its law. The power of sin is the law (Mortal law) (1 Cor. 15:56). This is the shove which starts the ball of evil to roll—it cannot move of itself.

God is my strength and power, and he maketh my way perfect.   2 Sam. 22:33.

Among those whom we are told to shun, are they who have a form of godliness, but deny the power thereof (2 Tim. 3:5). Look for spiritual help from those only who have assumed the whole command of Christ as their obligation (Matt. 10:7-8).

I can do all things through Christ which strengtheneth me.   Phil. 4:13.

You have as much power in any direction as you have the ability to grasp. It all depends upon yourself; the clearness of your spiritual vision, the purity of your thought, your faith, your desire. In other words if you have the Mind of the Spirit, you will know that all power is yours because you are connected with its source; but if you have the "mind of the flesh," you will see limitations and not beyond them, and your desire and capacity for power will be accordingly limited.

☞

Verily, verily, I say unto you; He that believeth on me, the works that I do shall he do also.
            John 14:12.

Do not listen to the voice of discouragement, it is never the voice of God. To say "I can't" is to deny the power of the Almighty—to blaspheme.

Thou madest him to have dominion over the works of thy hands; thou hast put all things under his feet: all sheep and oxen, yea, and the beasts of the field; the fowl of the air, and the fish of the sea, and whatsoever passeth through the paths of the seas. Ps. 8:6-8.

And to have power to heal sickness, and to cast out devils. Mark 3:15.

He giveth power to the faint; and to them that have no might he increaseth strength. Even the youths shall faint and be weary, and the young men shall utterly fall: But they that wait upon the Lord shall renew their strength; they shall mount up with wings as eagles; they shall run, and not be weary; and they shall walk, and not faint.

Isa. 40:29-31.

The flesh profiteth nothing. John 6:63.

The man who measures his ability by his physical strength cheats himself, he underestimates his working capital, he does not know "what manner of man he is," and he fails.

Both riches and honor come of thee, and thou reignest over all; and in thine hand is power and might; and in thine hand it is to make great, and to give strength unto all.

1 Chron. 29:12.

⌒

Neglect not the gift that is in thee.

1 Tim. 4:14.

When you become aware of the nature of this gift, when you discover the channel through which your particular message is to be delivered to the world, lend all of your energies to make the gift perfect and to keep the channel free of obstructions. Through this gift and this message, salvation will come to you as well as to others. You can have all the power in all ways, that you need; and you will have as much as you desire and seek for, if you live—not after the flesh, but after the spirit, looking to "the things that are above." Aim for perfection. Perfection is God. Remember, too, that this work which has been delegated to you to do, can be done by none other; therefore be faithful, be true. Trust.

Learn to do well.   Isa. 1:17.

Thou shalt remember the Lord thy God, for it is he that giveth thee power to get wealth.

Deut. 8:18.

Behold, I give unto you power to tread on serpents and scorpions, and over all the power of the enemy; and nothing shall by any means hurt you.

Luke 10:19.

That he would grant you, according to the riches of his glory, that ye may be strengthened with might by his Spirit in the inward man.   Eph. 3:16.

⌒

For the kingdom of God is not in word, but in power.   1 Cor. 4:20.

It is not in what you say, but in what you are able to demonstrate.

Seek the Lord, and his strength.   Ps. 105:4.

The people that do know their God shall be strong.
Dan. 11:32.

The way of the Lord is strength to the upright: but destruction shall be to the workers of iniquity.
Prov. 10:29.

Blessed is the man whose strength is in thee.
Ps. 84:5.

THE LORD SHALL GUIDE
THEE CONTINUALLY

Be still and know that I am God.   Ps. 46:10.

Never make plans while you are disturbed or troubled (Ps. 62:5). First "be still," then know that nothing can separate you from the love of God, and know, too, that harmonious conditions—always surrounding you—have not been manifesting themselves because of your state of mind. When there is truly inward peace, guidance will come. O Lord, I know that the way of man is not in himself; it is not in man that walketh to direct his steps (Jer. 10:23).

⌒

In all thy ways acknowledge him and he will make plain thy paths.

Prov. 3:6. (E.R.V.)

Be strong and of a good courage, fear not, nor be afraid of them; for the Lord thy God, he it is that doth go with thee; he will not fail thee, nor forsake thee.

Deut. 31:6.

Delight thyself also in the Lord and he shall give thee the desires of thine heart.

Ps. 37:4.

With thanksgiving let your requests be made known unto God.

Phil. 4:6.

Rejoice in the good that *has* come, and be thankful. Obedience to these two commands brings about meekness and humility, essentials to true receptivity (Ps. 37:11, first clause).

The meek will he guide in judgment: and the meek will he teach his way.

Ps. 25:9.

Set your mind on the things that are above, not upon the things that are upon the earth.

Col. 3:2.

My help cometh from the Lord (Ps. 121:2). Vain is the help of man (Ps. 60:11 and 108:12). Put on humbleness of mind (Col. 3:12). Have as your background your faith in the wisdom and knowledge of the Lord, and *know* that you will be guided aright. Neither be ye of doubtful mind (Luke 12:20). He will beautify the meek with victory (Ps. 149:4).

Commit thy way unto the Lord; trust also in him and he shall bring it to pass.

Ps. 37:5.

Seek ye first the kingdom of God (Matt. 6:33). Set your mind upon the limitless power which is at hand. Be patient and be assured that the Spirit in you leads to but one goal—your peace and happiness. If you set your mind upon things of the earth—the chaotic material world, you will have to have much strength to keep from being discouraged, from fretting and becoming impatient, all of which will weaken your faith and make obstructions in your path to success.

Commit thy works unto the Lord, and thy purposes shall be established.   Prov. 16:3. (E.R.V.)

The Lord shall guide thee continually.

Isa. 58:11.

Be not afraid of sudden fear, neither of the desolation of the wicked, when it cometh. For the Lord shall be thy confidence, and shall keep thy foot from being taken.

Prov. 3:25-26.

Not by might, nor by power, but by my Spirit, saith the Lord of hosts.

Zech. 4:6.

For he hath said, I will never leave thee, nor forsake thee.

Heb. 13:5.

He that is perfect in knowledge is with thee.

Job 36:4.

God is with thee in all that thou doest.

Gen. 21:22.

The Lord is nigh unto all them that call upon him, to all that call upon him in truth. He will fulfill the desire of them that fear him, he also will hear their cry and will save them. The Lord preserveth all them that love him.

Ps. 145:18-20.

I am the Lord thy God which teacheth thee to profit, which leadeth thee by the way that thou shouldest go.   Isa. 48:17.

I will instruct thee and teach thee in the way which thou shalt go; I will counsel thee with mine eye upon thee.   Ps. 32:8. (E.R.V.)

I will bring the blind by a way that they know not; in paths that they know not will I lead them; I will make darkness light before them, and crooked places straight. These things will I do, and I will not forsake them.   Isa. 42:16. (E.R.V.)

A man's goings are established of the Lord; and he delighteth in his way.   Ps. 37:23.

A man's heart deviseth his way; but the Lord directeth his steps.   Prov. 16:9.

Thy word is a lamp unto my feet, and light unto my path.   Ps. 119:105.

O Lord, I know that the way of man is not in himself; it is not in man that walketh to direct his steps.   Jer. 10:23.

But the path of the righteous is as the light of dawn, that shineth more and more unto the perfect day.

Prov. 4:18. (E.R.V.)

The way of the wicked is as darkness: they know not at what they stumble.

Prov. 4:19. (E.R.V.)

It is God that girdeth me with strength and maketh my way perfect.

Ps. 18:32.

The way of the righteous is made plain.

Prov. 15:19.

The righteousness of the perfect shall direct his way. But the wicked shall fall by his own wickedness.

Prov. 11:5.

He guideth my way in perfectness.

2 Sam. 22:33. (E.R.V.)

And thine ear shall hear a word behind thee, saying, this is the way, walk ye in it.

Isa. 30:21.

In righteousness shall thou be established; thou shalt be far from oppression, for thou shalt not fear; and from terror, for it shall not come near thee.

Isa. 54:14.

For with thee is the fountain of life; in thy light shall we see light.

Ps. 36:9.

The steps of a good man are ordered by the Lord: and he delighteth in his way.

Ps. 37:23.

It shall be told thee what thou must do.

Acts 9:6.

The Lord will lighten my darkness.

2 Sam. 22:29.

The Lord knoweth the days of the upright: and their inheritance shall be for ever. They shall not be ashamed in the evil time: and in the days of famine they shall be satisfied. But the wicked shall perish, and the enemies of the Lord shall be as the fat of lambs: they shall consume; into smoke shall they consume away.

Ps. 37:18-20.

Unto the upright there ariseth light in darkness.

Ps. 112:4.

⌒

Howbeit, when he, the Spirit of truth is come, he will guide you into all truth.

John 16:13.

And the Spirit of the Lord shall rest upon him, the spirit of wisdom and understanding, the spirit of counsel and might, the spirit of knowledge and of the fear of the Lord. And shall make him of quick understanding in the fear of the Lord; and he shall not judge after the sight of his eyes, neither reprove after the hearing of his ears.

Isa. 11:2-3.

Settle it therefore in your hearts, not to meditate before what ye shall answer, for I will give thou a mouth and wisdom, which all your adversaries shall not be able to gainsay nor resist.

Luke 21:14-15.

I have put my words in thy mouth, and I have covered thee in the shadow of mine hand.

Isa. 51:16.

The plans of the heart belong to man, but the answer of the tongue is from the Lord.

Prov. 16:1.

The sun shall be no more thy light by day; neither for brightness shall the moon give light unto thee: but the Lord shall be unto thee an everlasting light, and thy God thy glory. Thy sun shall no more go down; neither shall thy moon withdraw itself: for the Lord shall be thine everlasting light, and the days of thy mourning shall be ended. Thy people also shall be all righteous: they shall inherit the land for ever, the branch of my planting, the work of my hands, that I may be glorified. A little one shall become a thousand, and a small one a strong nation: I the Lord will hasten it in his time.

Isa. 6:19-22.

THOU SHALT WALK IN
THY WAY SAFELY

Whoso keepeth the commandment shall know no
evil thing.   Eccl. 8:5. (E.R.V.)

The eternal God is thy dwelling place, and under-
neath are the everlasting arms.
                              Deut. 33:27. (E.R.V.)

No one has the daring to deny that there is a power
protecting and caring for him. This much is uni-
versally admitted. But more is revealed to the
seeker after truth; he knows that this power is from
the Creator, the One, the only Power (Rom. 13:1),
therefore limitless; and he firmly believes—one
must believe, must *know*—that as easily as the river
carries the little bark down the stream, so will the
Spirit carry him on its bosom throughout all of his
experiences.

For all this I considered in my heart even to declare all this, that the righteous, and the wise, and their works, are in the hand of God.

Eccl. 9:1.

The ungodly are not so; but are like the chaff which the wind driveth away.

Ps. 1:4.

⌒

My help cometh from the Lord, which made heaven and earth.

Ps. 121:2.

Then shalt thou walk in thy way safely, and thy foot shall not stumble.

Prov. 3:23.

There shall not an hair of your head perish.

Luke 21:18.

⌒

He that loveth his brother abideth in the light, and there is none occasion of stumbling in him.

1 John 2:10.

Righteousness delivereth from death.

Prov. 10:2.

Set your affection on things above, not on things
on the earth.

Col. 3:2.

But whoso hearkeneth unto me shall dwell securely, and shall be quiet without fear of evil.

Prov. 1:33. (E.R.V.)

For thou hast delivered my soul from death, mine
eyes from tears, and my feet from falling.

Ps. 116:8.

Thou hast enlarged my steps under me; so that my
feet did not slip.

2 Sam. 22:37.

There shall no mischief happen to the righteous.
But the wicked shall be filled with evil.

Prov. 12:21.

A thousand shall fall at thy side, and ten thousand
at thy right hand; but it shall not come nigh thee.

Ps. 91:7.

For he shall give his angels charge over thee, to keep thee in all thy ways.

Ps. 91:11.

☞

The Lord is my shepherd; I shall not want. He maketh me to lie down in green pastures; he leadeth me beside the still waters. He restoreth my soul: he leadeth me in paths of righteousness for his name's sake. Yea, though I walk through the valley of the shadow of death, I will fear no evil; for thou art with me; thy rod and thy staff they comfort me. Thou preparest a table before me in the presence of mine enemies; thou anointest my head with oil; my cup runneth over. Surely goodness and mercy shall follow me all the days of my life: and I will dwell in the house of the Lord forever.

Ps. 23.

There is no king saved by the multitude of a host. A mighty man is not delivered by much strength. A horse is a vain thing for safety; neither doth he deliver any by his great strength.

Ps. 33:16-17.

I beheld the Lord always before my face; for he is on my right hand, that I should not be moved.

Acts 2:25. (E.R.V.)

Behold, the eye of the Lord is upon them that fear him, upon them that wait for his mercy to deliver their soul from death, and to keep them alive in famine.

Ps. 33:18-19.

☞

Even to old age I am he, and even to hoar hairs will I carry you: I have made, and I will bear; even, I will carry, and will deliver you.

Isa. 46:4.

The beloved of the Lord shall dwell in safety by him. He covereth him all the day long, and he dwelleth between his shoulders.

Deut. 33:12. (E.R.V.)

If I take the wings of the morning, and dwell in the uttermost parts of the sea; even there shall thy hand lead me, and thy right hand shall hold me.

Ps. 139:9-10.

I have covered thee in the shadow of mine hand.

Isa. 51:16.

Thus saith God the Lord, he that created the heavens, and stretched them out; he that spread forth the earth, and that which cometh out of it; he that giveth breath unto the people upon it, and spirit to them that walk therein: I the Lord have called thee in righteousness, and will hold thine hand, and will keep thee.

Isa. 42:5-6.

How excellent is thy lovingkindness, O God! Therefore the children of men put their trust under the shadow of thy wings.

Ps. 36:7.

ALL THINGS ARE YOURS

The Lord is my shepherd, I shall not want.

Ps. 23:1.

All things work together for good to them that love God.

Rom. 8:28.

No good thing will he withhold from them that walk uprightly.

Ps. 84:11.

Let not your heart be troubled; believe in God; believe also in me.

John 14:1. (E.R.V.)

Keep and seek for all of the commandments of the Lord, your God.

1 Chron. 28:8.

Only in this way will you gain understanding without which mortal man is adrift upon a tempestuous sea.

☙

Ye shall walk in all the ways which the Lord your God hath commanded you, that ye may live, and that it may be well with you, and that ye may prolong your days in the land which ye shall possess.

Deut. 5:33.

Wherefore ye shall do my statutes and keep my judgments and do them; and ye shall dwell in the land in safety. And the land shall yield its fruit, and ye shall eat your fill, and dwell therein in safety.

Lev. 25:18-19.

Poverty and shame shall be to him that refuseth instruction.

Prov. 13:18.

Ask and ye shall receive.

John 16:24.

You shall receive if you ask aright, submitting your will to God, who does all for your welfare and happiness (James 4:2-4).

In the morning sow thy seed, and in the evening withhold not thy hand; for thou knowest not which shall prosper, whether this or that, or whether they both shall be alike good.

Eccl. 11:6. (E.R.V.)

Do your best at all times. Do not let your faith make you lazy. Get understanding and you will learn why you should be busy with mind and hand. But he that looketh unto the perfect law, the law of liberty, and so continueth, being not a hearer that forgetteth but a doer that worketh, this man shall be blessed in his doing.

(James 1:25, E.R.V.).

☞

Be not therefore anxious, saying, What shall we eat? or, What shall we drink? Or Wherewithal shall we be clothed? For after all these things do the Gentiles seek; for your heavenly Father knoweth that ye have need of all these things. But seek ye first his kingdom, and his righteousness; and all these things shall be added unto you.

Matt. 6:31-33. (E.R.V.)

Consider the lilies how they grow: they toil not, they spin not: and yet I say unto you, that Solomon in all his glory was not arrayed like one of these. If then God so clothe the grass which is today in the field, and tomorrow is cast into the oven; how much more will he clothe you, O ye of little faith? And seek not ye what ye shall eat, or what ye shall drink, neither be ye of doubtful mind. For all these things do the nations of the world seek after; and your Father knoweth that ye have need of these things. But rather seek ye the kingdom of God; and all these things shall be added unto you.

Luke 12:27-31.

Eliminate worry; it is a veil that hides the good that is everywhere about you. Trust in the Lord and do good, so shalt thou dwell in the land and verily thou shalt be fed.

(Ps. 37:3).

Acquaint now thyself with him, and be at peace; thereby good shall come unto thee.

Job 22:21.

Delight thyself also in the Lord; and he shall give thee the desires of thine heart. Commit thy way unto the Lord; trust also in him; and he shall bring it to pass.

Ps. 37:4-5.

⮜

If thou return to the Almighty thou shalt be built up; if thou put away unrighteousness far from thy tents. And lay thou thy treasure in the dust, and the gold of Ophir among the stones of the brooks; and the Almighty will be thy treasure, and precious silver unto thee. For then shalt thou delight thyself in the Almighty and shalt lift up thy face unto God. Thou shalt make thy prayer unto him and he will hear thee; and thou shalt pay thy vows. Thou shalt also decree a thing and it shall be established unto thee; and light shall shine upon thy ways.

Job 22:23-28. (E.R.V.)

Charge them that are rich in this world, that they be not high minded, nor trust in uncertain riches, but in the living God, who giveth us richly all things to enjoy.

1 Tim. 6:17.

And it shall come to pass, if ye shall hearken diligently unto my commandments which I command you this day, to love the Lord your God, and to serve him with all your heart and with all your soul, that I will give you the rain of your land in its due season, the first rain and the latter rain, that thou mayest gather in thy corn, and thy wine, and thine oil. And I will send grass in thy fields for thy cattle, that thou mayest eat and be full. Take heed to yourselves, that your heart be not deceived, and ye turn aside, and serve other gods, and worship them.

Deut. 11:13-16.

☞

By humility and the fear of the Lord are riches, and honor, and life.

Prov. 22:4.

I am become rich, I have found me out substance.

Hosea 12:8.

Riches and honor are with me: yea, durable riches and righteousness.

Prov. 8:18.

In the house of the righteous is much treasure.

Prov. 15:6.

I am the Lord, thy God, who teacheth thee to profit.

Isa. 48:17.

He hath filled the hungry with good things.

Luke 1:53.

The blessing of Jehovah, it maketh rich; toil addeth nothing thereto.

Prov. 10:22. (E.R.V.)

They shall prosper that love thee. Peace be within thy walls, and prosperity within thy palaces.

Ps. 122:6-7.

A man can receive nothing, except it be given him from heaven.

John 3:27.

Take heed, and keep yourselves from all covetousness: for a man's life consisteth not in the abundance of the things which he possesseth.

Luke 12:15. (E.R.V.)

Wisdom and knowledge is granted unto thee; and will give thee riches, and wealth, and honor.

2 Chron. 1:12.

But to each one is given the manifestation of the Spirit to profit withal.

1 Cor. 12:7. (E.R.V.)

Godliness is profitable unto all things.

1 Tim. 4:8.

⌒

They that seek the Lord shall not want any good thing.

Ps. 34:10.

State the truth that all good is yours, deny the belief that anything can interfere with it and it will become manifest in all your affairs.

Our sufficiency is of God.

2 Cor. 3:5.

Except the Lord build the house, they labor in vain that build it: Except the Lord keep the city, the watchman waketh but in vain. It is vain for you that ye rise up early, and so late take rest, And eat of the bread of toil: For so he giveth unto his beloved in sleep.

Ps. 127:1-2. (E.R.V.)

⟡

Give me neither poverty nor riches. Feed me with the food that is needful for me.

Prov. 30:8. (E.R.V.)

Blessed is every one that feareth the Lord: that walketh in his ways. For thou shalt eat the labor of thine hands: Happy shalt thou be, and it shall be well with thee.

Ps. 128:1-2.

He that trusteth in his riches shall fall; but the righteous shall flourish as the branch.

Prov. 11:28.

⟡

Behold that which I have seen; it is good and comely for one to eat and to drink, and to enjoy the good of all his labor that he taketh under the sun all the days of his life, which God giveth him, for it is his portion. Every man also to whom God hath given riches and wealth, and hath given him power to eat thereof, and to take his portion, and to rejoice in his labor; this is the gift of God. For he shall not much remember the days of his life, because God answereth him in the joy of his heart.

Eccl. 5:18-20.

I know that there is nothing better for them, than to rejoice, and to get good so long as they live. And also that every man should eat and drink and enjoy good in all his labor, is the gift of God.

Eccl. 3:12-13. (E.R.V.)

And they shall build houses, and inhabit them; and they shall plant vineyards, and eat the fruit of them. They shall not build, and another inhabit; they shall not plant, and another eat; for as the days of a tree are the days of my people, and mine elect shall long enjoy the work of their hands. They shall not labor in vain, nor bring forth for trouble; for they are the seed of the blessed of the Lord, and their offspring with them.

Isa. 65:21-23.

And the Lord will guide thee continually, and
satisfy thy soul in drought, and make fat thy bones;
and thou shalt be like a watered garden, and like a
spring of water, whose waters fail not.

Isa. 58:11.

There is a sore evil which I have seen under the
sun, namely, riches kept for the owners thereof to
their hurt.

Eccl. 5:13.

☞

If ye be willing and obedient, ye shall eat the good
of the land.

Isa. 1:19.

If they hearken and serve him, they shall spend
their days in prosperity, and their years in pleasantness.

Job 36:11. (E.R.V.)

Praise ye the Lord. Blessed is the man that feareth
the Lord, that delighteth greatly in his commandments. His seed shall be mighty upon earth; the
generation of the upright shall be blessed. Wealth

and riches shall be in his house; and his righteousness endureth forever.

Ps. 112:1-3.

Blessed is the man that trusteth in the Lord, and whose hope the Lord is. For he shall be as a tree planted by the waters, and that spreadeth out her roots by the river, and shall not see when heat cometh, but her leaf shall be green; and shall not be careful in the year of drought, neither shall cease from yielding fruit.

Jer. 17:7-8.

Every good giving and every perfect boon is from above, coming down from the Father of Lights with whom can be no variation, neither shadow that is cast by turning.

James 1:17. (E.R.V.)

For he satisfieth the longing soul, and the hungry soul he filleth with good.

Ps. 107:9. (E.R.V.)

The righteous shall inherit the land and dwell therein forever.

Ps. 37:29.

I walk in the way of righteousness, in the midst of the paths of judgment. That I may cause those that love me to inherit substance; and I will fill their treasuries.

Prov. 8:20-21.

Your iniquities have turned away these things, and your sins have withholden good things from you.

Jer. 5:25.

Yea, the Lord shall give that which is good; and our land shall yield her increase.

Ps. 85:12.

Then shalt thou see and be lightened, and thy heart shall tremble and be enlarged; because the abundance of the sea shall be turned unto thee, the wealth of the nations shall come unto thee.

Isa. 60:5.

While the earth remaineth, seed time and harvest, and cold and heat, and summer and winter, and day and night shall not cease.

Gen. 8:22.

If ye walk in my statutes, and keep my commandments, and do them; then I will give you rain in due season, and the land shall yield her increase, and the trees of the field shall yield their fruit. And your threshing shall reach unto the vintage, and the vintage shall reach unto the sowing time; and ye shall eat your bread to the full, and dwell in your land safely.

Lev. 26:3-5.

We can no more keep good from coming to us if we are consciously at one with the Almighty, than we can hold the tide back with our hands.

I have been young, and now am old; yet have I not seen the righteous forsaken, nor his seed begging bread.

Ps. 37:25.

Hold fast to the thought that there is an abundance for each, "more than one can ask or think." One might as well hold one's breath for fear that the air will be exhausted, as to be fearful that the supply will be diminished because a few have amassed great fortunes.

Happy is the man that walketh not in the counsel of the wicked, nor standeth in the way of sinners, nor sitteth in the seat of scoffers. But his delight is in the law of the Lord, and in his law doth he meditate day and night. And he shall be like a tree planted by the streams of water, that bringeth forth its fruit in its season. Whose leaf also doth not wither, and in whatsoever he doeth he shall prosper.

Ps. 1:1-3.

The ungodly are not so, but are like the chaff which the wind driveth away.

Ps. 1:4.

The righteous giveth and spareth not.

Prov. 21:26.

All things are yours.

1 Cor. 3:21.

Just as the sunbeam draws forth from the sun its light and warmth, so does the child of God (the divine ray) draw forth from the divine nature all that is needful.

Both riches and honor come of thee, and thou reignest over all; and in thine hand is power and might; and in thine hand it is to make great, and to give strength unto all. Now, therefore, our God, we thank thee, and praise thy glorious name.

1 Chron. 29:12-13.

☙

Eye hath not seen, nor ear heard, neither have entered into the heart of man, the things which God hath prepared for them that love him.

1 Cor. 2:9.

PEACE BE UNTO YOU

The fruit of the Spirit is love, joy, peace, long suffering, kindness, goodness, faithfulness, meekness, self-control.

Gal. 5:22-23. (E.R.V.)

Therefore love the truth and peace.

Zech. 8:19.

For all this I considered in my heart, even to declare all this, that the righteous, and the wise, and their works, are in the hand of God (Eccl. 9:1). This verse is enough to bring perfect peace to one with understanding.

Live in peace.

2 Cor. 13:11.

Depart from evil, and do good; seek peace, and pursue it.

Ps. 34:14.

When thou drawest nigh unto a city to fight against it, then proclaim peace unto it.

Deut. 20:10.

And into whatever house ye enter, first say: Peace be to this house.

Luke 10:5.

Let us therefore follow after the things which make for peace, and things wherewith one may edify another.

Rom. 14:19.

Have peace one with another.

Mark 9:50.

When you feel irritable force yourself to do a kind act; it will let Love into your consciousness, and that means peace.

Blessed are the peacemakers.

Matt. 5:9.

Follow peace with all men, and holiness, without which no man shall see the Lord.

Heb. 12:14.

And follow after righteousness, faith, love, peace, with them that call on the Lord out of a pure heart.
2 Tim. 2:22. (E.R.V.)

And let the peace of God rule in your hearts, to the which also ye are called in one body; and be ye thankful.

Col. 3:15.

Acquaint now thyself with him, and be at peace, thereby good shall come unto thee.

Job 22:21.

When he giveth quietness, who then can make trouble?

Job 34:29.

For God is not the author of confusion, but of peace.

1 Cor. 14:33.

Peace, be still.

Mark 4:39.

Remember, when you seem to be helpless in the midst of confusion, that your real self abides in eternal harmony, and that it is possible for you to manifest this harmony under all circumstances if you but put behind you the thought that confusion is real and can harm you. Understand that there is no power in evil other than that which our thoughts give to it.

For thus saith the Lord God, the Holy One of Israel; in returning and rest shall ye be saved; in quietness and in confidence shall be your strength.

Isa. 30:15.

Be not therefore anxious for the morrow: for the morrow will be anxious for itself. Sufficient unto the day is the evil thereof.

Matt. 6:34. (E.R.V.)

Come unto me, all ye that labor, and are heavy laden, and I will give you rest. Take my yoke upon you, and learn of me; for I am meek and lowly in heart, and ye shall find rest unto your souls. For my yoke is easy, and my burden is light.

Matt. 11:28-30.

Endeavoring to keep the unity of the Spirit in the bond of peace.

Eph. 4:3.

Thou wilt keep him in perfect peace, whose mind is stayed on thee: because he trusteth in thee.

Isa. 26:3.

☞

Mark the perfect man, and behold the upright; for there is a reward for the man of peace.

Ps. 37:37. (E.R.V.)

But whoso hearkeneth unto me shall dwell securely, and shall be quiet without fear of evil.

Prov. 1:33. (E.R.V.)

Now the God of hope fill you with all joy and peace in believing, that ye may abound in hope, through the power of the Holy Ghost.

Rom. 15:13.

Thou shalt increase my greatness, and comfort me on every side.

Ps. 71:21.

The Lord will give strength unto his people; the Lord will bless his people with peace.

Ps. 29:11.

Peace I leave with you, my peace I give unto you;
not as the world giveth, give I unto you. Let not
your heart be troubled, neither let it be afraid.

John 14:27.

Great peace have they that love thy law; and they
have no occasion of stumbling.

Ps. 119:165. (E.R.V.)

The eternal, unchanging Law of God meets every
condition. He who has understanding knows this,
and the knowledge brings him peace.

What man is he that feareth the Lord? Him shall
he teach in the way that he shall choose. His soul
shall dwell at ease.

Ps. 25:12-13.

To whom he said, this is the rest wherewith ye may
cause the weary to rest; and this is the refreshing.

Isa. 28:12.

For I know the thoughts that I think toward you,
saith the Lord, thoughts of peace, and not of evil,
to give you hope in your latter end.

Jer. 29:11.

To give light to them that sit in darkness and in the shadow of death, to guide our feet into the way of peace.

Luke 1:79.

These things I have spoken unto you, that in me ye may have peace. In the world ye shall have tribulation; but be of good cheer; I have overcome the world.

John 16:33.

But the meek shall inherit the earth, and shall delight themselves in the abundance of peace.

Ps. 37:11.

But glory, and honor and peace to every man that worketh good.

Rom. 2:10.

When a man's ways please the Lord, he maketh even his enemies to be at peace with him. Better is a little with righteousness than great revenues without right.

Prov. 16:7-8.

In this place will I give peace, saith the Lord of hosts.

Hag. 2:9.

Blessed is the man that walketh not in the counsel of the ungodly, nor standeth in the way of sinners, nor sitteth in the seat of the scornful. But his delight is in the law of the Lord; and in his law doth he meditate day and night.

Ps. 1:1-2.

O that thou hadst hearkened to my commandments, then had thy peace been as a river, and thy righteousness as the waves of the sea.

Isa. 48:18.

And the work of righteousness shall be peace; and the effect of righteousness, quietness and assurance forever. And my people shall dwell in a peaceable habitation and in sure dwellings, and in quiet resting places.

Isa. 32:17-18.

The wolf also shall dwell with the lamb, and the leopard shall lie down with the kid; and the calf and the young lion and the fatling together; and a little child shall lead them. And the cow and the bear shall feed; their young ones shall lie down together; and the lion shall eat straw like the ox. And the sucking child shall play on the hole of the asp, and the weaned child shall put his hand on the cockatrice den. They shall not hurt nor destroy in all my holy mountain; for the earth shall be full of the knowledge of the Lord, as the waters cover the sea.

Isa. 11:6-9.

⮌

The mountains shall bring peace to the people, and the little hills, by righteousness.

Ps. 72:3.

The whole earth is at rest, and is quiet; they break forth into singing.

Isa. 14:7.

For thou shalt be in league with the stones of the field; and the beasts of the field shall be at peace with thee; and thou shalt know that thy tabernacle shall be in peace; and thou shalt visit thy habitation, and shalt not sin.

Job 5:23-24.

Now the Lord of peace himself give you peace at all times in all ways. The Lord be with you all.

2 Thes. 3:16. (E.R.V.)

Glory to God in the highest, and on earth peace, good will toward men.

Luke 2:14.

☞

And the peace of God, which passeth all under-standing, shall guard your hearts and your thoughts in Christ Jesus.

Phil. 4:7. (E.R.V.)

HAPPY SHALT THOU BE

Whoso trusteth in the Lord, happy is he.

Prov. 16:20.

Happiness, like health, harmony and peace, is the normal, eternal condition of the real, the Spiritual Man. It belongs entirely to the kingdom of the Spirit, for happiness is a state of being, and there can be no such state for the one who believes in the power of the flesh and the material world, for such a one has allied himself to the fleeting and the ever changing—to perpetual death—and must ever be in a state of fear.

He that keepeth the law, happy is he.

Prov. 29:18.

The selfish man builds about him a prison house which narrows and darkens as the years go by until at last he is smothered in its black confines.

But he that looketh into the perfect law, the law of
liberty, and so continueth, being not a hearer that
forgetteth, but a doer that worketh, this man shall
be blessed in his doing.

James 1:25. (E.R.V.)

～

I am come that they might have life, and that they
might have it more abundantly.

John 10:10.

Blessed is the man whose strength is in thee, in
whose heart are the highways to Zion. Passing
through the valley of weeping they make it a place
of springs: yea, the early rain covereth it with
blessings. They go from strength to strength.

Ps. 84:5-7.

But the path of the righteous is as the light of
dawn, that shineth more and more unto the perfect
day.

Prov. 4:18. (E.R.V.)

In the way of righteousness is life; and in the
pathway thereof there is no death.

Prov. 12:28.

And they shall come and sing in the height of Zion, and shall flow together unto the goodness of the Lord, to the corn, and to the wine, and to the oil, and to the young of the flock and of the herd: and their soul shall be as a watered garden; and they shall not sorrow any more at all.

Jer. 31:12.

⌒

Then shalt thou see and be lightened, and thine heart shall tremble and be enlarged; because the abundance of the sea shall be turned unto thee, the wealth of the nations shall come unto thee.

Isa. 60:5. (E.R.V.)

The world desires happiness above everything else, and is willing to work hard for whatever will bring it. You as a Christian believe that it comes only through spiritual understanding, and you will *live* your profession if you are a true Christian. The world will want none of your faith if you go around morose or sad, or with a sour countenance. On the other hand a wonderful way to magnify God in the eyes of men is to radiate from your face the sunlight of His love.

To him that overcometh, to him will I give to eat of the tree of life, which is in the garden of God.

Rev. 2:7. (E.R.V.)

Blessed is everyone that feareth the Lord, that walketh in his ways. For thou shalt eat the labor of thine hands: happy shalt thou be, and it shall be well with thee.

Ps. 128:1.

Then I commended mirth, because a man hath no better thing under the sun, than to eat, and to drink, and to be merry: and that this should accompany him in his labor all the days of his life which God hath given him under the sun.

Eccl. 8:15. (E.R.V.)

Go thy way, eat thy bread with joy, and drink thy wine with a merry heart; for God now accepteth thy works.

Eccl. 9:7.

Thou wilt show me the path of life: in thy presence is fulness of joy: at thy right hand there are pleasures for evermore.

Ps. 16:11.

In famine he shall redeem thee from death: and in war from the power of the sword. Thou shalt be hid

from the scourge of the tongue: neither shalt thou
be afraid of destruction when it cometh. At destruction and famine thou shalt laugh; neither shall
thou be afraid of the beasts of the earth.

Job 5:20-22.

☙

The hope of the righteous shall be gladness.

Prov. 10:28.

Make me to hear joy and gladness.

Ps. 51:8.

☙

Therefore did my heart rejoice, and my tongue was
glad; moreover also my flesh shall rest in hope.

Acts 2:26.

But the sorrow of the world worketh death.

2 Cor. 7:10.

Thou madest known unto me the ways of life; thou
shalt make me full of gladness in thy presence.

Acts 2:28. (E.R.V.)

Thou hast put gladness in my heart, more than they have when their corn and their wine are increased.

Ps. 4:7.

A man's gift maketh room for him, and bringeth him before great men.

Prov. 18:16.

Arise, shine; for thy light is come, and the glory of the Lord is risen upon thee. For, behold, the darkness shall cover the earth, and gross darkness the people: but the Lord shall rise upon thee and his glory shall be seen upon thee.

Isa. 60:1-2.

For joy is withered away from the sons of men (Joel 1:12). Our happiest moments are always those that have resulted from spiritual activity: such as when we have been unselfish; have given of ourselves (Isa. 58:10); after we have established peace between those who have misunderstood each other (Matt. 5:9); or have manifested God through loving attention to the unfortunate; or, which is harder, to the disagreeable person; or to him who lacks in any way—in other words to the poor (Prov. 14:21, last clause). If we are true through such experiences as these, the resultant satisfaction is the distilled joy of Heaven.

～

He that walketh righteously, and speaketh uprightly; he that despiseth the gain of fraud, that shaketh his hands from holding of bribes, that stoppeth his ears from hearing of blood, and shutteth his eyes from looking upon evil; he shall dwell on high; his place of defense shall be the munitions of rocks; his bread shall be given him; his waters shall be sure.

Isa. 33:15-16.

Do not find fault nor comment upon anything but the good unless it is absolutely necessary. Shut your eyes to all so-called, unavoidable evil, which includes the disagreeable, the disappointing, the imperfect, sin, disease and death. Never idly or uselessly complain. Be thankful that you slept as well as you did last night. To complain is to bring upon yourself further unrest and cause confusion in the minds of others.

Evil of itself is powerless to do harm, being unreal. A ball, no matter how perfect a sphere, never of itself starts to roll. We usually conduct ourselves as though we believed the reverse, and as our beliefs control us we are harmed.

⌒

The spirit of the Lord God is upon me; because the Lord hath anointed me to preach good tidings unto the meek; he hath sent me to bind up the broken-hearted, to proclaim liberty to the captives, and the opening of the prison to them that are bound; to proclaim the acceptable year of the Lord; . . . to comfort all that mourn; to appoint unto them that mourn in Zion—to give unto them a garland for ashes, the oil of joy for mourning, the garment of praise for the spirit of heaviness; that they might be called trees of righteousness, the planting of the Lord that he might be glorified.

Isa. 61:1–3. (E.R.V.)

Praise ye the Lord. Blessed is the man that feareth the Lord, that delighteth greatly in his commandments. His seed shall be mighty upon earth: the generation of the upright shall be blessed. Wealth and riches shall be in his house; and his righteousness endureth forever.

Ps. 112:1-3.

Thou madest him to have dominion over the works of thy hands; thou hast put all things under his feet.

Ps. 8:6.

All the paths of the Lord are lovingkindness and truth unto such as keep his covenant and his testimonies.

Ps. 25:10.

Unto the upright there ariseth light in the darkness: he is gracious and full of compassion, and righteous. Well is it with the man that dealeth graciously and lendeth; he shall maintain his cause in judgment. For he shall never be moved; the righteous shall be had in everlasting remembrance. He shall not be afraid of evil tidings: his heart is fixed, trusting in the Lord. His heart is established, he shall not be afraid until he sees his desire upon his adversaries. He hath dispersed, he hath given to the needy; his righteousness endureth for ever: his horn shall be exalted with honor.

Ps. 112:4-9. (E.R.V.)

The Lord will perfect that which concerneth me.

Ps. 138:8.

Violence shall no more be heard in thy land,
desolation nor destruction within thy borders; but
thou shalt call thy walls Salvation and thy gates
Praise. The sun shall be no more thy light by day;
neither for brightness shall the moon give light
unto thee: but the Lord will be unto thee an everlasting light, and thy God thy beauty . . . and the
days of thy mourning shall be ended. Thy people
also shall be all righteous; they shall inherit the
land for ever, the branch of my planting, the work
of my hands, that I may be glorified. The little one
shall become a thousand, and the small one a
strong nation: I the Lord will hasten it in its time.

Isa. 60:18-22. (E.R.V.)

☞

He will swallow up death in victory; and the Lord
God will wipe away tears from off all faces.

Isa. 25:8.

O death, where is thy sting? O grave, where is thy
victory?

1 Cor. 15:55.

To him with understanding the death of the body
is not the occasion of despairing grief, for he knows

that Life and Love are deathless—not of the flesh, but of God. He does not look upon the prism as sparkling of itself, but sees playing upon it the sunbeam that shines on unchanged even thou the prism disappears. So to him the disappearance of the fleshly body does not mean the loss nor the separation of the dear one, for he knows that this dear one still lives and asks for love, and in turn loves and serves better than ever before, because he has come into his own, and is unfettered—free. Unfortunately many of us are idolaters, we love the fleshly body of the dear one to the exclusion of everything else, and when it disappears we are as though we had lost our all, and we refuse to be comforted.

☙

He shall wipe away every tear from their eyes; and death shall be no more; neither shall there be mourning, nor crying, nor pain, any more: the first things are passed away.

Rev. 21:4. (E.R.V.)

Therefore the redeemed of the Lord shall return, and come with singing unto Zion; and everlasting joy shall be upon their head: they shall obtain gladness and joy: and sorrow and mourning shall flee away.

Isa. 51:11.

For the Lord shall comfort Zion; he will comfort all her waste places; and he will make her wilderness like Eden, and her desert like the garden of the Lord; joy and gladness shall be found therein, thanksgiving, and the voice of melody.

Isa. 51:3.

THE LORD WILL LIGHTEN
MY DARKNESS

Rejoice in the Lord.

Phil. 4:4.

Giving thanks always for all things unto God and the Father in the name of our Lord Jesus Christ.

Eph. 5:20.

With thanksgiving let your requests be made known unto God.

Phil. 4:6.

☙

For so he giveth unto his beloved in sleep.

Ps. 127:2. (E.R.V.)

Before you are ready to close your eyes in sleep be sure that you are not holding anything unlovely in your consciousness—anything unlike God. Laying aside every fear put yourself entirely in His charge. Quiet yourself with the thought that He who has all power protects you, gives you health and all else that you need, in abundance; and know that whether sleeping or waking you are safe because your life is hid with Christ in God (Col. 3:3).

For God speaketh in one way, yea, in two, though man regardeth it not. In a dream, in a vision of the night when deep sleep falleth upon men, in slumberings upon the bed. Then he openeth the ears of men, and sealeth their instruction, that he may withdraw man from his purpose, and hide pride from man. That he may keep back his soul from the pit, and his life from perishing by the sword.

Job 33:14-18. (E.R.V.)

And the peace of God which passeth all understanding, shall keep your hearts and minds through Christ Jesus.

Phil. 4:7.

Commune with your own heart upon your bed, and be still.

Ps. 4:4.

Thy word is a lamp unto my feet, and a light unto my path.

Ps. 119:105.

The opening of thy words giveth light; it giveth understanding unto the simple.

Ps. 119:130.

For thou art my lamp, O Lord: and the Lord will lighten my darkness.

2 Sam. 22:29.

In peace will I both lay me down and sleep, for thou the Lord alone makest me dwell in safety.

Ps. 4:8. (E.R.V.)

My presence shall go with thee, and I will give thee rest.

Ex. 33:14.

Thou shalt be secure, because there is hope; . . . and thou shalt take thy rest in safety.

Job 11:18.

They shall rest in their beds.

Isa. 57:2.

I laid me down and slept; I awaked; for the Lord sustaineth me.

Ps. 3:5.

⌒

Thou shalt not be afraid for the terror by night.

Ps. 91:5.

Also thou shalt lie down, and none shall make thee afraid; yea, many shall make suit unto thee.

Job 11:19.

When thou liest down, thou shalt not be afraid: yea, thou shalt lie down, and thy sleep shall be sweet.

Prov. 3:24.

The day is thine, the night also is thine: thou hast prepared the light and the sun. Thou hast set all the borders of the earth: thou has made summer and winter.

Ps. 74:16-17.

If I take the wings of the morning, and dwell in the uttermost parts of the sea; even there shall thy

hand lead me, and thy right hand shall hold me. If
I say, surely the darkness shall overwhelm me, and
the light about me shall be night; even in the
darkness hideth not from thee, but the night
shineth as the day: The darkness and the light are
both alike to thee.

Ps. 139:9-12. (E.R.V)

☞

Ye shall have a song, as in the night when a holy
solemnity is kept; and gladness of heart, as when
one goeth with a pipe to come into the mountain of
the Lord, to the Mighty One of Israel.

Isa. 30:29.

My soul shall be satisfied as with marrow and
fatness; and my mouth shall praise thee with joyful
lips: when I remember thee upon my bed, and
meditate on thee in the night-watches.

Ps. 63:5-6.

For then shalt thou have thy delight in the Almighty, and shalt lift up thy face unto God. Thou
shalt make thy prayer unto him, and he shall hear
thee, and thou shalt pay thy vows. Thou shalt also

decree a thing, and it shall be established unto thee: and the light shall shine upon thy ways.

Job 22:26-28.

And I will give peace in the land and ye shall lie down, and none shall make you afraid.

Lev. 26:6.

For thou shalt forget thy misery; thou shalt remember it as waters that are passed away, and thy life shall be clearer than the noonday; though there be darkness, it shall be as the morning. And thou shalt be secure, because there is hope; yea, thou shalt search about thee, and shalt take thy rest in safety.

Job 11:16-18.

It is a good thing to give thanks unto the Lord and sing praises unto thy name, O Most High: To show forth thy lovingkindness in the morning, and thy faithfulness every night.

Ps. 92:1-2.

Yet the Lord will command his lovingkindness in the daytime, and in the night his song shall be with me, and my prayer unto the God of my life.

Ps. 42:8.

O Lord, in the morning shalt thou hear my voice. In the morning will I order my prayer unto thee, and will keep watch.

Ps. 5:3. (E.R.V.)

Cause me to hear thy lovingkindness in the morning; for in thee do I trust. Cause me to know the way wherein I should walk; for I lift up my soul unto thee. Teach me to do thy will; for thou art my God. Thy Spirit is good.

Ps. 143:8, 10.